FREE Test Taking Tips DVD Offer

To help us better serve you, we have developed a Test Taking Tips DVD that we would like to give you for FREE. **This DVD covers world-class test taking tips that you can use to be even more successful when you are taking your test.**

All that we ask is that you email us your feedback about your study guide. Please let us know what you thought about it – whether that is good, bad or indifferent.

To get your **FREE Test Taking Tips DVD**, email freedvd@studyguideteam.com with "FREE DVD" in the subject line and the following information in the body of the email:

   a. The title of your study guide.

   b. Your product rating on a scale of 1-5, with 5 being the highest rating.

   c. Your feedback about the study guide. What did you think of it?

   d. Your full name and shipping address to send your free DVD.

If you have any questions or concerns, please don't hesitate to contact us at freedvd@studyguideteam.com.

Thanks again!

SSAT Middle Level Prep Book

Study Guide & Practice Book for the Middle Level SSAT Exam

Test Prep Books Middle School Practice Book Team

Table of Contents

Formulas:

Area: $L \times W$

Volume: $L \times W \times H$

Area of Triangle: Base $\times$ Height $\times \frac{1}{2}$

Circumference $= 2\pi r$ or πd

Area of circle $= \pi r^2$

Angle of Tri. add to 180

——● $= 360°$

——●—— $= 180$

○———→ >

●———→ >

Quick Overview

As you draw closer to taking your exam, effective preparation becomes more and more important. Thankfully, you have this study guide to help you get ready. Use this guide to help keep your studying on track and refer to it often.

This study guide contains several key sections that will help you be successful on your exam. The guide contains tips for what you should do the night before and the day of the test. Also included are test-taking tips. Knowing the right information is not always enough. Many well-prepared test takers struggle with exams. These tips will help equip you to accurately read, assess, and answer test questions.

A large part of the guide is devoted to showing you what content to expect on the exam and to helping you better understand that content. Near the end of this guide is a practice test so that you can see how well you have grasped the content. Then, answer explanations are provided so that you can understand why you missed certain questions.

Don't try to cram the night before you take your exam. This is not a wise strategy for a few reasons. First, your retention of the information will be low. Your time would be better used by reviewing information you already know rather than trying to learn a lot of new information. Second, you will likely become stressed as you try to gain a large amount of knowledge in a short amount of time. Third, you will be depriving yourself of sleep. So be sure to go to bed at a reasonable time the night before. Being well-rested helps you focus and remain calm.

Be sure to eat a substantial breakfast the morning of the exam. If you are taking the exam in the afternoon, be sure to have a good lunch as well. Being hungry is distracting and can make it difficult to focus. You have hopefully spent lots of time preparing for the exam. Don't let an empty stomach get in the way of success!

When travelling to the testing center, leave earlier than needed. That way, you have a buffer in case you experience any delays. This will help you remain calm and will keep you from missing your appointment time at the testing center.

Be sure to pace yourself during the exam. Don't try to rush through the exam. There is no need to risk performing poorly on the exam just so you can leave the testing center early. Allow yourself to use all of the allotted time if needed.

Remain positive while taking the exam even if you feel like you are performing poorly. Thinking about the content you should have mastered will not help you perform better on the exam.

Once the exam is complete, take some time to relax. Even if you feel that you need to take the exam again, you will be well served by some down time before you begin studying again. It's often easier to convince yourself to study if you know that it will come with a reward!

Test-Taking Strategies

1. Predicting the Answer

When you feel confident in your preparation for a multiple-choice test, try predicting the answer before reading the answer choices. This is especially useful on questions that test objective factual knowledge or that ask you to fill in a blank. By predicting the answer before reading the available choices, you eliminate the possibility that you will be distracted or led astray by an incorrect answer choice. You will feel more confident in your selection if you read the question, predict the answer, and then find your prediction among the answer choices. After using this strategy, be sure to still read all of the answer choices carefully and completely. If you feel unprepared, you should not attempt to predict the answers. This would be a waste of time and an opportunity for your mind to wander in the wrong direction.

2. Reading the Whole Question

Too often, test takers scan a multiple-choice question, recognize a few familiar words, and immediately jump to the answer choices. Test authors are aware of this common impatience, and they will sometimes prey upon it. For instance, a test author might subtly turn the question into a negative, or he or she might redirect the focus of the question right at the end. The only way to avoid falling into these traps is to read the entirety of the question carefully before reading the answer choices.

3. Looking for Wrong Answers

Long and complicated multiple-choice questions can be intimidating. One way to simplify a difficult multiple-choice question is to eliminate all of the answer choices that are clearly wrong. In most sets of answers, there will be at least one selection that can be dismissed right away. If the test is administered on paper, the test taker could draw a line through it to indicate that it may be ignored; otherwise, the test taker will have to perform this operation mentally or on scratch paper. In either case, once the obviously incorrect answers have been eliminated, the remaining choices may be considered. Sometimes identifying the clearly wrong answers will give the test taker some information about the correct answer. For instance, if one of the remaining answer choices is a direct opposite of one of the eliminated answer choices, it may well be the correct answer. The opposite of obviously wrong is obviously right! Of course, this is not always the case. Some answers are obviously incorrect simply because they are irrelevant to the question being asked. Still, identifying and eliminating some incorrect answer choices is a good way to simplify a multiple-choice question.

4. Don't Overanalyze

Anxious test takers often overanalyze questions. When you are nervous, your brain will often run wild, causing you to make associations and discover clues that don't actually exist. If you feel that this may be a problem for you, do whatever you can to slow down during the test. Try taking a deep breath or counting to ten. As you read and consider the question, restrict yourself to the particular words used by the author. Avoid thought tangents about what the author *really* meant, or what he or she was *trying* to say. The only things that matter on a multiple-choice test are the words that are actually in the question. You must avoid reading too much into a multiple-choice question, or supposing that the writer meant something other than what he or she wrote.

5. No Need for Panic

It is wise to learn as many strategies as possible before taking a multiple-choice test, but it is likely that you will come across a few questions for which you simply don't know the answer. In this situation, avoid panicking. Because most multiple-choice tests include dozens of questions, the relative value of a single wrong answer is small. Moreover, your failure on one question has no effect on your success elsewhere on the test. As much as possible, you should compartmentalize each question on a multiple-choice test. In other words, you should not allow your feelings about one question to affect your success on the others. When you find a question that you either don't understand or don't know how to answer, just take a deep breath and do your best. Read the entire question slowly and carefully. Try rephrasing the question a couple of different ways. Then, read all of the answer choices carefully. After eliminating obviously wrong answers, make a selection and move on to the next question.

6. Confusing Answer Choices

When working on a difficult multiple-choice question, there may be a tendency to focus on the answer choices that are the easiest to understand. Many people, whether consciously or not, gravitate to the answer choices that require the least concentration, knowledge, and memory. This is a mistake. When you come across an answer choice that is confusing, you should give it extra attention. A question might be confusing because you do not know the subject matter to which it refers. If this is the case, don't eliminate the answer before you have affirmatively settled on another. When you come across an answer choice of this type, set it aside as you look at the remaining choices. If you can confidently assert that one of the other choices is correct, you can leave the confusing answer aside. Otherwise, you will need to take a moment to try to better understand the confusing answer choice. Rephrasing is one way to tease out the sense of a confusing answer choice.

7. Your First Instinct

Many people struggle with multiple-choice tests because they overthink the questions. If you have studied sufficiently for the test, you should be prepared to trust your first instinct once you have carefully and completely read the question and all of the answer choices. There is a great deal of research suggesting that the mind can come to the correct conclusion very quickly once it has obtained all of the relevant information. At times, it may seem to you as if your intuition is working faster even than your reasoning mind. This may in fact be true. The knowledge you obtain while studying may be retrieved from your subconscious before you have a chance to work out the associations that support it. Verify your instinct by working out the reasons that it should be trusted.

8. Key Words

Many test takers struggle with multiple-choice questions because they have poor reading comprehension skills. Quickly reading and understanding a multiple-choice question requires a mixture of skill and experience. To help with this, try jotting down a few key words and phrases on a piece of scrap paper. Doing this concentrates the process of reading and forces the mind to weigh the relative importance of the question's parts. In selecting words and phrases to write down, the test taker thinks about the question more deeply and carefully. This is especially true for multiple-choice questions that are preceded by a long prompt.

9. Subtle Negatives

One of the oldest tricks in the multiple-choice test writer's book is to subtly reverse the meaning of a question with a word like *not* or *except*. If you are not paying attention to each word in the question, you can easily be led astray by this trick. For instance, a common question format is, "Which of the following is...?" Obviously, if the question instead is, "Which of the following is not...?," then the answer will be quite different. Even worse, the test makers are aware of the potential for this mistake and will include one answer choice that would be correct if the question were not negated or reversed. A test taker who misses the reversal will find what he or she believes to be a correct answer and will be so confident that he or she will fail to reread the question and discover the original error. The only way to avoid this is to practice a wide variety of multiple-choice questions and to pay close attention to each and every word.

10. Reading Every Answer Choice

It may seem obvious, but you should always read every one of the answer choices! Too many test takers fall into the habit of scanning the question and assuming that they understand the question because they recognize a few key words. From there, they pick the first answer choice that answers the question they believe they have read. Test takers who read all of the answer choices might discover that one of the latter answer choices is actually *more* correct. Moreover, reading all of the answer choices can remind you of facts related to the question that can help you arrive at the correct answer. Sometimes, a misstatement or incorrect detail in one of the latter answer choices will trigger your memory of the subject and will enable you to find the right answer. Failing to read all of the answer choices is like not reading all of the items on a restaurant menu: you might miss out on the perfect choice.

11. Spot the Hedges

One of the keys to success on multiple-choice tests is paying close attention to every word. This is never more true than with words like *almost, most, some,* and *sometimes.* These words are called "hedges" because they indicate that a statement is not totally true or not true in every place and time. An absolute statement will contain no hedges, but in many subjects, like literature and history, the answers are not always straightforward or absolute. There are always exceptions to the rules in these subjects. For this reason, you should favor those multiple-choice questions that contain hedging language. The presence of qualifying words indicates that the author is taking special care with his or her words, which is certainly important when composing the right answer. After all, there are many ways to be wrong, but there is only one way to be right! For this reason, it is wise to avoid answers that are absolute when taking a multiple-choice test. An absolute answer is one that says things are either all one way or all another. They often include words like *every, always, best,* and *never.* If you are taking a multiple-choice test in a subject that doesn't lend itself to absolute answers, be on your guard if you see any of these words.

12. Long Answers

In many subject areas, the answers are not simple. As already mentioned, the right answer often requires hedges. Another common feature of the answers to a complex or subjective question are qualifying clauses, which are groups of words that subtly modify the meaning of the sentence. If the question or answer choice describes a rule to which there are exceptions or the subject matter is complicated, ambiguous, or confusing, the correct answer will require many words in order to be expressed clearly and accurately. In essence, you should not be deterred by answer choices that seem excessively long. Oftentimes, the author of the text will not be able to write the correct answer without offering some qualifications and modifications. Your job is to read the answer choices thoroughly and completely and to select the one that most accurately and precisely answers the question.

13. Restating to Understand

Sometimes, a question on a multiple-choice test is difficult not because of what it asks but because of how it is written. If this is the case, restate the question or answer choice in different words. This process serves a couple of important purposes. First, it forces you to concentrate on the core of the question. In order to rephrase the question accurately, you have to understand it well. Rephrasing the question will concentrate your mind on the key words and ideas. Second, it will present the information to your mind in a fresh way. This process may trigger your memory and render some useful scrap of information picked up while studying.

14. True Statements

Sometimes an answer choice will be true in itself, but it does not answer the question. This is one of the main reasons why it is essential to read the question carefully and completely before proceeding to the answer choices. Too often, test takers skip ahead to the answer choices and look for true statements. Having found one of these, they are content to select it without reference to the question above. Obviously, this provides an easy way for test makers to play tricks. The savvy test taker will always read the entire question before turning to the answer choices. Then, having settled on a correct answer choice, he or she will refer to the original question and ensure that the selected answer is relevant. The mistake of choosing a correct-but-irrelevant answer choice is especially common on questions related to specific pieces of objective knowledge, like historical or scientific facts. A prepared test taker will have a wealth of factual knowledge at his or her disposal, and should not be careless in its application.

15. No Patterns

One of the more dangerous ideas that circulates about multiple-choice tests is that the correct answers tend to fall into patterns. These erroneous ideas range from a belief that B and C are the most common right answers, to the idea that an unprepared test-taker should answer "A-B-A-C-A-D-A-B-A." It cannot be emphasized enough that pattern-seeking of this type is exactly the WRONG way to approach a multiple-choice test. To begin with, it is highly unlikely that the test maker will plot the correct answers according to some predetermined pattern. The questions are scrambled and delivered in a random order. Furthermore, even if the test maker was following a pattern in the assignation of correct answers, there is no reason why the test taker would know which pattern he or she was using. Any attempt to discern a pattern in the answer choices is a waste of time and a distraction from the real work of taking the test. A test taker would be much better served by extra preparation before the test than by reliance on a pattern in the answers.

FREE DVD OFFER

Don't forget that doing well on your exam includes both understanding the test content and understanding how to use what you know to do well on the test. We offer a completely FREE Test Taking Tips DVD that covers world class test taking tips that you can use to be even more successful when you are taking your test.

All that we ask is that you email us your feedback about your study guide. To get your **FREE Test Taking Tips DVD**, email freedvd@studyguideteam.com with "FREE DVD" in the subject line and the following information in the body of the email:

    a.   The title of your study guide.
    b.   Your product rating on a scale of 1-5, with 5 being the highest rating.
    c.   Your feedback about the study guide. What did you think of it?
    d.   Your full name and shipping address to send your free DVD.

Introduction

Function of the Test

The Secondary School Admission Test (SSAT) is a standardized test used for students that are applying to an independent or private school. The Middle Level SSAT is administered to students currently in grades 5 through 7, applying to grades 6 through 8, and it evaluates math, reading, and verbal skills. The test is used in the US and is also available in several other countries throughout the world to determine if students have the necessary skills for success in a college preparatory program.

The SSAT is administered in a standard testing format and a Flex testing format. The standard SSAT is administered on 8 specific dates throughout the year, while the Flex test is administered to a student on any other date than the standard test. The Flex test is administered by an educational consultant or school at the student's request.

Test Administration

The standard SSAT is offered on 8 Saturdays throughout the year. The standard test is available at hundreds of testing centers in the US and locations throughout the world. Sunday testing is available for religious reasons, but must be approved before registration. Students may repeat the standard test without penalty. Students must create an account on the SSAT website in order to register. This account also allows students to print their admission tickets and receive their test scores. Registration opens about 10 weeks prior to a testing date. Late registration begins 3 weeks before the test date and rush registration starts 10 days before the test date. Late and rush registrations incur additional fees.

Students who cannot attend the standard test dates can opt to take the Flex test. The Flex test may be provided in an open or closed format. A school may administer an open Flex test on a date other than the standard test for all registrants. The closed format is administered in a small group or individually at as school with an educational consultant. Students may only take the Flex SSAT once in an academic year.

Testing accommodations are available for students with disabilities. Students requiring accommodations must apply and be approved before registering for the test. Approval is only required once in an academic year.

Test Format

The Middle Level SSAT consists of multiple-choice questions in Quantitative (Math), Verbal, Reading Comprehension, and Experimental sections, and a writing sample. The writing sample is not scored, but is sent to prospective schools for assessment of a student's writing ability.

The writing sample asks the student to choose between two creative writing prompts and to write an original story based on the prompt. The Quantitative section is broken down into two parts, each with 25 questions in the areas of number concepts, geometry, algebra, and probability. The Verbal section includes 60 questions: 30 on synonyms and 30 analogies. The Reading Comprehension section includes a total of 40 questions relating to several short passages. These questions focus mainly on reading comprehension skills, including inferences, identifying the main idea, and determining the author's purpose. The Experimental section includes 16 questions in the Verbal, Reading, and Quantitative areas in order to test their reliability for SSAT forms to be used in the future. The Experimental section is not scored. The testing period and sections are broken down as follows:

Section	Questions	Question Type	Time Allotted
Writing Sample	1	Written Response	25 minutes
Break			5 minutes
Quantitative (Part 1)	25	Multiple Choice	30 minutes
Reading	40	Multiple Choice	40 minutes
Break			10 minutes
Verbal	60	Multiple Choice	30 minutes
Quantitative (Part 2)	25	Multiple Choice	30 minutes
Experimental	16	Multiple Choice	15 minutes

Scoring

In the Middle Level SSAT, students are given one point for each correct answer, and they lose a quarter of a point for each incorrect answer. Unanswered questions do not affect the score either way.

A free scoring report is available online through a student's SSAT account roughly 2 weeks after the test date. The report includes a narrative explanation of the scores, along with a raw score, a scaled score, percentile rank, and total scaled score. The possible scaled score ranges from 440 – 710 per section, and the percentile rank is from 1 – 99. The total scaled score range is 1320 – 2130, with a mid-point of 1725.

The SSAT is a norm-referenced test, meaning that the score is compared to a norm group of test takers' scores from the last 3 years. The score report includes the student's scores, as well as the average norm scores in each section for comparison. The percentile rank shows how a student performed relative to the norm group. For example, if a student's percentile is 80, it means he or she scored the same or better than 80% of those in the norm group. Schools use many factors to select students for admission, so a "good score" or passing score is difficult to determine.

Recent/Future Developments

The SSAT testing accommodations were updated in the 2016-2017 academic year. The official guidelines for accommodations can be accessed on the SSAT.org website.

Writing Sample

The Middle Level SSAT begins with a 25-mintue writing sample section where test takers are asked to write a creative story based on one of two prompts to choose from. While this section is not scored, the writing sample can be provided with the score report to each admission's office for an additional fee. This section gives test takers the opportunity to show their writing ability as well as demonstrate creativity and self-expression. Test takers should be sure that their stories have a beginning, middle, and end.

Planning should occur after looking at the picture or reading the prompt but before beginning any writing. This brainstorming stage is when writers consider their purpose and think of ideas that they can use in their writing. Graphic organizers like story webs are excellent tools to use during the planning stage. Graphic organizers can help connect the writing purpose to supporting details, and they can help begin the process of structuring the writing piece.

POWER Strategy for Writing

The POWER strategy helps writers focus and be successful during the writing process.

The POWER strategy stands for the following:

- Prewriting or Planning
- Organizing
- Writing a first draft
- Evaluating the writing
- Revising and rewriting

Prewriting
During the Prewriting and Planning phase, writers learn to consider their audience and purpose for the writing assignment. Then they compile information they wish to include in the piece of writing from their background knowledge and/or new sources.

Organizing
Next, writers decide on the organizational structure of their writing project. There are many types of organizational structures, but the common ones are: story/narrative, informative, opinion, persuasive, compare and contrast, explanatory, and problem/solution formats.

Writing
The following are characteristics that make writing readable and effective no matter what genre of writing is being used:

- Ideas
- Organization
- Voice
- Word choice
- Sentence fluency
- Proper Writing Conventions
- Presentation

Ideas

This refers to the content of the writing. Writers should select an important topic for their writing or focus correctly on the topic depicted in the picture or prompt. They should narrow down and focus their idea, remembering that during the test, they only have fifteen minutes to plan and write, and that time can go quickly! Then they learn to develop and elaborate on the specific idea and choose the information and details that best convey the idea to others.

Organization

Many writers, especially during a test, are inclined to jump into their writing without a clear direction for where it is going. Organization helps plan a successful piece of writing.

Writers must choose an organizational strategy or purpose for the writing and build the details upon that structure. There are many purposes for writing, and they all have slightly different frameworks. Writers can learn to effectively organize their writing so it makes sense to the reader.

- Introduction (beginning): Writers should invite the reader into their work with an effective introduction. They should restate the prompt or topic sentence in their own words so that readers know what they are going to read about.
- Body (middle): The body is where the main thoughts and ideas that were developed during brainstorming are put together. Thoughtful transitions between ideas and key points help keep readers engaged and understanding. Writers should create logical and purposeful sequences of ideas.
- Conclusion (end): Writers should include a powerful conclusion to their piece that summarizes the information but leaves the reader with something to think about.

Voice

This characteristic gives the writing a sense of individuality and connection to the author. It shows that the writing is meaningful and that the author cares about it. It is what makes the writing uniquely the author's own. It is how the reader begins to know the author and what he or she "sounds like."

Word Choice

The right word choice helps an author communicate his or her ideas in a text that is clear, rich, and enjoyable for readers. If the work is narrative, the words create images in the mind's eye. If the work is descriptive, the words clarify and expand thoughts and ideas. If the work is an opinion piece, the words give new perspective and invite thought. Writers should choose descriptive vocabulary and language that is accurate, concise, precise, and lively.

Sentence Fluency

When sentences are built to fit together and move with one another to create writing that is easy to read aloud, the author has written with fluency. Sentences and paragraphs start and stop in just the right places so that the writing moves well. Sentences should have a variety of structures and lengths.

Proper Writing Conventions

Writers should make their writing clear and understandable through the use of proper grammar, spelling, capitalization, and punctuation.

Presentation

Writers should try to make their work inviting and accessible to the reader of the end product. Writers show they care about their writing when it is neat and readable.

<u>Evaluating</u>

In this stage, writers reread the writing and note the segments that are particularly strong or need improvement.

<u>Revising and Rewriting</u>

Finally, the writer incorporates any changes he or she wishes to make based on the evaluating process. Then writers rewrite the piece into a final draft however it best fits the audience and purpose of the writing.

Tips for the Writing Section

- Don't panic! This section isn't scored. It's just a great way to show teachers how smart you are and how well you can tell a story and write. You can do it!
- Use your time well. Fifteen minutes is quick! It is shorter than almost every TV show. Don't spend too much time doing any one thing. Try to brainstorm briefly and then get writing. Leave a few minutes to read it over and correct any spelling mistakes or confusing parts.
- Be yourself! You are smart and interesting and teachers want to get to know you and your unique ideas. Don't feel pressured to use big vocabulary words if you aren't positive what they mean. You will be more understandable if you use the right word, not the fanciest word.

Practice Writing Sample

Select one of the following two-story starters and write a creative story in the space provided. Make sure that your story has a beginning, middle, and end and is interesting for readers.

- The snow continued to fall for four full days.
- I waited and waited but my luggage did not make it off the plane.

Quantitative Reasoning

Number Concepts and Operations

Arithmetic Word Problems (Percent, Ratio)

Word problems present the opportunity to relate mathematical concepts learned in the classroom into real-world situations. These types of problems are situations in which some parts of the problem are known and at least one part is unknown.

There are three types of instances in which something can be unknown: the starting point, the modification, or the final result can all be missing from the provided information.

- For an addition problem, the modification is the quantity of a new amount added to the starting point.
- For a subtraction problem, the modification is the quantity taken away from the starting point.

Keywords in the word problems can signal what type of operation needs to be used to solve the problem. Words such as *total, increased, combined,* and *more* indicate that addition is needed. Words such as *difference, decreased,* and *minus* indicate that subtraction is needed.

Regarding addition, the given equation is $3 + 7 = 10$.

The number 3 is the starting point. 7 is the modification, and 10 is the result from adding a new amount to the starting point. Different word problems can arise from this same equation, depending on which value is the unknown. For example, here are three problems:

- If a boy had three pencils and was given seven more, how many would he have in total?
- If a boy had three pencils and a girl gave him more so that he had ten in total, how many was he given?
- A boy was given seven pencils so that he had ten in total. How many did he start with?

All three problems involve the same equation, and determining which part of the equation is missing is the key to solving each word problem. The missing answers would be 10, 7, and 3, respectively.

In terms of subtraction, the same three scenarios can occur. The given equation is $6 - 4 = 2$.

The number 6 is the starting point. 4 is the modification, and 2 is the new amount that is the result from taking away an amount from the starting point. Again, different types of word problems can arise from this equation. For example, here are three possible problems:

- If a girl had six quarters and two were taken away, how many would be left over?
- If a girl had six quarters, purchased a pencil, and had two quarters left over, how many did she pay with?
- If a girl paid for a pencil with four quarters and had two quarters left over, how many did she have to start with?

The three question types follow the structure of the addition word problems, and determining whether the starting point, the modification, or the final result is missing is the goal in solving the problem. The missing answers would be 2, 4, and 6, respectively.

The three addition problems and the three subtraction word problems can be solved by using a picture, a number line, or an algebraic equation. If an equation is used, a question mark can be utilized to represent the unknown quantity. For example, $6 - 4 = ?$ can be written to show that the missing value is the result. Using equation form visually indicates what portion of the addition or subtraction problem is the missing value.

Similar instances can be seen in word problems involving multiplication and division. Key words within a multiplication problem involve *times, product, doubled,* and *tripled.* Key words within a division problem involve *split, quotient, divided, shared, groups,* and *half.* Like addition and subtraction, multiplication and division problems also have three different types of missing values.

Multiplication consists of a specific number of groups having the same size, the quantity of items within each group, and the total quantity within all groups. Therefore, each one of these amounts can be the missing value.

For example, the given equation is $5 \times 3 = 15$.

5 and 3 are interchangeable, so either amount can be the number of groups or the quantity of items within each group. 15 is the total number of items. Again, different types of word problems can arise from this equation. For example, here are three problems:

- If a classroom is serving 5 different types of apples for lunch and has three apples of each type, how many total apples are there to give to the students?
- If a classroom has 15 apples with 5 different types, how many of each type are there?
- If a classroom has 15 apples with 3 of each type, how many types are there to choose from?

Each question involves using the same equation to solve, and it is imperative to decide which part of the equation is the missing value. The answers to the problems are 15, 3, and 5, respectively.

Similar to multiplication, division problems involve a total amount, a number of groups having the same size, and a number of items within each group. The difference between multiplication and division is that the starting point is the total amount, which then gets divided into equal quantities.

For example, the equation is $15 \div 5 = 3$.

15 is the total number of items, which is being divided into 5 different groups. In order to do so, 3 items go into each group. Also, 5 and 3 are interchangeable, so the 15 items could be divided into 3 groups of 5 items each. Therefore, different types of word problems can arise from this equation depending on which value is unknown. For example, here are three types of problems:

- A boy needs 48 pieces of chalk. If there are 8 pieces in each box, how many boxes should he buy?
- A boy has 48 pieces of chalk. If each box has 6 pieces in it, how many boxes did he buy?
- A boy has partitioned all of his chalk into 8 piles, with 6 pieces in each pile. How many pieces does he have in total?

Each one of these questions involves the same equation, and the third question can easily utilize the multiplication equation $8 \times 6 = ?$ instead of division. The answers are 6, 8, and 48, respectively.

Word problems can appear daunting, but don't let the verbiage psyche you out. No matter the scenario or specifics, the key to answering them is to translate the words into a math problem. Always keep in mind what the question is asking and what operations could lead to that answer.

Word problems involving elapsed time, money, length, volume, and mass require:

- determining which operations (addition, subtraction, multiplication, and division) should be performed, and
- using and/or converting the proper unit for the scenario.

The following table lists key words which can be used to indicate the proper operation:

Addition	Sum, total, in all, combined, increase of, more than, added to
Subtraction	Difference, change, remaining, less than, decreased by
Multiplication	Product, times, twice, triple, each
Division	Quotient, goes into, per, evenly, divided by half, divided by third, split

Identifying and utilizing the proper units for the scenario requires knowing how to apply the conversion rates for money, length, volume, and mass. For example, given a scenario which requires subtracting 8 inches from $2\frac{1}{2}$ feet, both values should first be expressed in the same unit (they could be expressed $\frac{2}{3}$ft & $2\frac{1}{2}$ft, or 8in and 30in). The desired unit for the answer may also require converting back to another unit.

Consider the following scenario: A parking area along the river is only wide enough to fit one row of cars and is $\frac{1}{2}$ kilometers long. The average space needed per car is 5 meters. How many cars can be parked along the river? First, all measurements should be converted to similar units: $\frac{1}{2}$km = 500m. The operation(s) needed should be identified. Because the problem asks for the number of cars, the total space should be divided by the space per car. Five-hundred meters divided by five meters per car yields a total of 100 cars. Written as an expression, the meters unit cancels and the cars unit is left: $\frac{500m}{5m/car}$ the same as $500m \times \frac{1\ car}{5m}$ yields 100 cars.

When dealing with problems involving elapsed time, breaking the problem down into workable parts is helpful. For example, suppose the length of time between 1:15pm and 3:45pm must be determined. From 1:15pm to 2:00pm is 45 minutes (knowing there are 60 minutes in an hour). From 2:00pm to 3:00pm is 1 hour. From 3:00pm to 3:45pm is 45 minutes. The total elapsed time is 45 minutes plus 1 hour plus 45 minutes. This sum produces 1 hour and 90 minutes. 90 minutes is over an hour, so this is converted to1 hour (60 minutes) and 30 minutes. The total elapsed time can now be expressed as 2 hours and 30 minutes.

The following word problems highlight the most commonly tested question types.

Working with Money

Walter's Coffee Shop sells a variety of drinks and breakfast treats.

Price List		Costs	
Hot Coffee	$2.00	Hot Coffee	$0.25
Slow Drip Iced Coffee	$3.00	Slow Drip Iced Coffee	$0.75
Latte	$4.00	Latte	$1.00
Muffins	$2.00	Muffins	$1.00
Crepe	$4.00	Crepe	$2.00
Egg Sandwich	$5.00	Egg Sandwich	$3.00

Walter's utilities, rent, and labor costs him $500 per day. Today, Walter sold 200 hot coffees, 100 slow drip iced coffees, 50 lattes, 75 muffins, 45 crepes, and 60 egg sandwiches. What was Walter's total profit today?

To accurately answer this type of question, determine the total cost of making his drinks and treats, then determine how much revenue he earned from selling those products. After arriving at these two totals, the profit is measured by deducting the total cost from the total revenue.

Walter's costs for today:

Item	Quantity	Cost Per Unit	Total Cost
Hot Coffee	200	$0.25	$50
Slow-Drip Iced Coffee	100	$0.75	$75
Latte	50	$1.00	$50
Muffin	75	$1.00	$75
Crepe	45	$2.00	$90
Egg Sandwich	60	$3.00	$180
Utilities, rent, and labor			$500
Total Costs			$1,020

Walter's revenue for today:

Item	Quantity	Revenue Per Unit	Total Revenue
Hot Coffee	200	$2.00	$400
Slow-Drip Iced Coffee	100	$3.00	$300
Latte	50	$4.00	$200
Muffin	75	$2.00	$150
Crepe	45	$4.00	$180
Egg Sandwich	60	$5.00	$300
Total Revenue			$1,530

Walter's Profit = $Revenue - Costs$ = $1,530 - $1,020 = $510

This strategy is applicable to other question types. For example, calculating salary after deductions, balancing a checkbook, and calculating a dinner bill are common word problems similar to business planning. Just remember to use the correct operations. When a balance is increased, use addition. When a balance is decreased, use subtraction. Common sense and organization are your greatest assets when answering word problems.

Unit Rate

Unit rate word problems will ask you to calculate the rate or quantity of something in a different value. For example, a problem might tell you that a car drove a certain number of miles in a certain number of minutes and then ask how many miles per hour the car was traveling. These questions involve solving proportions. Consider the following examples:

1) Alexandra made $96 during the first 3 hours of her shift as a temporary worker at a law office. She will continue to earn money at this rate until she finishes in 5 more hours. How much does Alexandra make per hour? How much will Alexandra have made at the end of the day?

This problem can be solved in two ways. The first is to set up a proportion, as the rate of pay is constant. The second is to determine her hourly rate, multiply the 5 hours by that rate, and then add the $96. We'll solve it using both methods.

To set up a proportion, put the money already earned over the hours already worked on one side of an equation. The other side has x over 8 hours (the total hours worked in the day). It looks like this: $\frac{96}{3} = \frac{x}{8}$. Now, cross-multiply to get $768 = 3x$. To get x, we divide by 3, which leaves us with $x = 256$. Thus, Alexandra will make $256 at the end of the day. To calculate her hourly rate, we need to divide the total by 8, giving us $32 per hour.

Alternatively, we could figure out the hourly rate by dividing $96 by 3 hours to get $32 per hour. Now we can figure out her total pay by multiplying $32 per hour by 8 hours, which comes out to $256.

2) Jonathan is reading a novel. So far, he has read 215 of the 335 total pages. It takes Jonathan 25 minutes to read 10 pages, and the rate is constant. How long does it take Jonathan to read one page? How much longer will it take him to finish the novel? Express the answer in time.

To calculate how long it takes Jonathan to read one page, we need to divide the 25 minutes by 10 pages to determine the page per minute rate. Thus, it takes 2.5 minutes to read one page.

Jonathan must read 120 more pages to complete the novel. (This is calculated by subtracting the pages already read from the total.) Now, we need to multiply his rate per page by the number of pages. Thus, $120 \times 2.5 = 300$. Expressed in time, 300 minutes is equal to 5 hours.

3) At a hotel, $\frac{4}{5}$ of the 120 rooms are booked for Saturday. On Sunday, $\frac{3}{4}$ of the 120 rooms are booked. On which day are more of the rooms booked, and by how much more?

The first step is to calculate the number of rooms booked for each day. We can do this by multiplying the fraction of the rooms booked by the total number of rooms.

$$\text{Saturday:} \frac{4}{5} \times 120 = \frac{4}{5} \times \frac{120}{1} = \frac{480}{5} = 96 \text{ rooms}$$

$$\text{Sunday:} \frac{3}{4} \times 120 = \frac{3}{4} \times \frac{120}{1} = \frac{360}{4} = 90 \text{ rooms}$$

Thus, more rooms were booked on Saturday by 6 rooms.

4) In a veterinary hospital, the veterinarian-to-pet ratio is 1:9. The ratio is always constant. If there are 45 pets in the hospital, how many veterinarians are currently in the veterinary hospital?

We can set up a proportion to solve for the number of veterinarians: $\frac{1}{9} = \frac{x}{45}$

After cross-multiplying, we're left with $9x = 45$, which works out to 5 veterinarians.

Alternatively, as there are always 9 times as many pets as veterinarians, we can divide the number of pets (45) by 9. This also arrives at the correct answer of 5 veterinarians.

5) At a general practice law firm, 30% of the lawyers work solely on tort cases. If 9 lawyers work solely on tort cases, how many lawyers work at the firm?

We need to solve for the total number of lawyers working at the firm, which we will represent with x. We know that 9 lawyers work solely on torts cases, and they make up 30% of the total lawyers at the firm. Thus, 30% multiplied by the total, x, will equal 9. Written as equation, this is: $30\% \times x = 9$.

It's easier to deal with the equation if we convert the percentage to a decimal, leaving us with $0.3x = 9$. Thus, $x = \frac{9}{0.3} = 30$ lawyers working at the firm.

6) Xavier was hospitalized with pneumonia. He was originally given 35mg of antibiotics. Later, after his condition continued to worsen, Xavier's dosage was increased to 60mg. What was the percent increase of the antibiotics? Round the percentage to the nearest tenth.

For questions asking for the increase in percentage, we need to calculate the difference, divide by the original amount, and multiply by 100. Written as an equation, the formula is: $\frac{new\ quanity\ -old\ quantity}{old\ quantity} \times$ 100. This formula also works if you are asked for the percentage decrease.

Here, the question tells us that the dosage increased from 35mg to 60mg, so we can plug those numbers into the formula to find the percentage increase.

$$\frac{60-35}{35} \times 100 \ = \frac{25}{35} \times 100 = .7142 \times 100 = 71.4\%$$

Basic Concepts of Addition, Subtraction, Multiplication, and Division

The four most basic and fundamental operations are addition, subtraction, multiplication, and division. The operations take a group of numbers and achieve an exact result, according to the operation. When dealing with positive integers greater than 1, addition and multiplication increase the result, while subtraction and division reduce the result.

Addition
Addition is the combination of two numbers so their quantities are added together cumulatively. The sign for an addition operation is the + symbol. For example, 9 + 6 = 15. The 9 and 6 combine to achieve a cumulative value, called a sum.

Addition holds the Commutative Property, which means that numbers in an addition equation can be switched without altering the result. The formula for the Commutative Property is $a + b = b + a$. Let's look at a few examples to see how the Commutative Property works:

$$3 + 4 = 4 + 3 = 7$$

$$12 + 8 = 8 + 12 = 20$$

Addition also holds the Associative Property, which means that the groups of numbers don't matter in an addition problem. The formula for the Associative Property is $(a + b) + c = a + (b + c)$. Here are some examples of the Associative Property at work:

$$(6 + 14) + 10 = 6 + (14 + 10) = 30$$

$$8 + (2 + 25) = (8 + 2) + 25 = 35$$

Subtraction
Subtraction is taking away one number from another, so their quantities are reduced. The sign designating a subtraction operation is the − symbol, and the result is called the difference. For example, $9 − 6 = 3$. The second number detracts from the first number in the equation to reach the difference.

Unlike addition, subtraction doesn't follow the Commutative or Associative Properties. The order and grouping in subtraction impacts the result.

$$22 - 7 \neq 7 - 22$$

$$(10 - 5) - 2 \neq 10 - (5 - 2)$$

When working through subtraction problems involving larger numbers, it's necessary to regroup the numbers. Let's work through a practice problem using regrouping:

$$325$$

$$-\quad 77$$

Here, we see that the ones and tens column for 77 is greater than 325. Thus, we need to borrow from the tens and hundreds column to complete the operation. When borrowing from a column, we subtract one digit from the lender and add ten to the borrower's column:

$$3\ 1\ 15$$

$$-\quad 7\ 7$$

$$2\ 11\ 15$$

$$-\quad 7\ 7$$

$$2\ 4\ 8$$

After ensuring greater numbers at the top of each column, we subtract as normal and arrive at the answer of 248.

Multiplication

Multiplication involves taking multiple copies of one number. The sign designating a multiplication operation is the x symbol. The result is called the product. For example, $9 \times 6 = 54$. Multiplication means adding together one number in the equation as many times as the number on the other side of the equation:

$$9 \times 6 = 9 + 9 + 9 + 9 + 9 + 9 = 54$$

$$9 \times 6 = 6 + 6 + 6 + 6 + 6 + 6 + 6 + 6 + 6 = 54$$

Like addition, multiplication holds the Commutative and Associative Properties:

$$2 \times 4 = 4 \times 2$$

$$2 \times 5 = 5 \times 20$$

$$(2 \times 4) \times 10 = 2x(4 \times 10)$$

$$3 \times (7 \times 4) = (3 \times 7) \times 4$$

Multiplication also follows the Distributive Property, which allows the multiplication to be distributed through parentheses. The formula for distribution is $a \times (b + c) = ab + ac$. This will become clearer after some examples:

$$5 \text{ x } (3 + 6) = (5 \text{ x } 3) + (5 \text{ x } 6) = 45$$

$$4 \text{ x } (10 - 5) = (4 \text{ x } 10) - (4 \text{ x } 5) = 20$$

Multiplication becomes slightly more complicated when multiplying numbers with decimals. The easiest way to answer these problems is to ignore the decimals and multiply as if they were whole numbers. After multiplying the factors, add a decimal point to the product, and the decimal place should be equal to the total number of decimal places in the problem. Here are two examples to familiarize you with the trick:

1.

$$\begin{array}{r} 0.7 \\ \times \quad 3 \\ \hline 2.1 \end{array}$$

2.

$$\begin{array}{r} 2.6 \\ \times \quad 4.2 \\ \hline 10.92 \end{array}$$

Let's tackle the first example. First, count the decimal places (one). Second, multiply the factors as if they were whole numbers to arrive at a product: 21. Finally, move the decimal place one position to the left, as the factors have only one decimal place. The second problem works the same exact away, except that there are two decimal places in the factors, so the product's decimal is moved two places over.

Division

Division is the opposite of multiplication as addition and subtraction are opposites. The signs designating a division operate are the ÷ or / symbols. In division, the second number divides the first. Like subtraction, it matters which number comes before the division sign. For example, $9 \div 6 \neq 6 \div 9$.

The number before the division sign is called the dividend, or, if expressed as a fraction, then it's the numerator. For example, in a ÷ b, a is the dividend. In $\frac{a}{b}$, a is the numerator.

The number after the division sign is called the **divisor**, or, if expressed as a fraction, then it's the denominator. For example, in a ÷ b, b is the divisor. In $\frac{a}{b}$, b is the denominator.

Division doesn't follow any of the Commutative, Associative, or Distributive Properties.

$$15 \div 3 \neq 3 \div 15$$

$$(30 \div 3) \div 5 \neq 30 \div (3 \div 5)$$

$$100 \div (20 + 10) \neq (100 \div 20) + (100 \div 10)$$

Division with decimals is similar to multiplication with decimals. When dividing a decimal by a whole number, ignore the decimal and divide as if it were a whole number. Once you solve for the answer (also called the *quotient*), then place the decimal at the decimal place equal to that in the dividend.

$$15.75 \div 3 = 5.25$$

When the divisor is a decimal, change it to a whole number by multiplying both the divisor and dividend by the factor of 10 that makes the divisor into a whole number. Then complete the division operation as described above.

$$17.5 \div 2.5 = 175 \div 25 = 7$$

Order of Operations

When reviewing calculations consisting of more than one operation, the order in which the operations are performed affects the resulting answer. Consider $5 \times 2 + 7$. Performing multiplication then addition results in an answer of 17 ($5 \times 2 = 10$; $10 + 7 = 17$). However, if the problem is written $5 \times (2 + 7)$, the order of operations dictates that the operation inside the parenthesis must be performed first. The resulting answer is $45 (2 + 7 = 9$, then $5 \times 9 = 45)$.

The order in which operations should be performed is remembered using the acronym PEMDAS. PEMDAS stands for parenthesis, exponents, multiplication/division, addition/subtraction. Multiplication and division are performed in the same step, working from left to right with whichever comes first. Addition and subtraction are performed in the same step, working from left to right with whichever comes first.

Consider the following example: $8 \div 4 + 8(7 - 7)$. Performing the operation inside the parenthesis produces $8 \div 4 + 8(0)$ or $8 \div 4 + 8 \times 0$. There are no exponents, so multiplication and division are performed next from left to right resulting in: $2 + 8 \times 0$, then $2 + 0$. Finally, addition and subtraction are performed to obtain an answer of 2. Now consider the following example: $6 \times 3 + 3^2 - 6$. Parenthesis are not applicable. Exponents are evaluated first, which brings us to $6 \times 3 + 9 - 6$. Then multiplication/division forms $18 + 9 - 6$. At last, addition/subtraction leads to the final answer of 21.

Properties of Operations

Properties of operations exist that make calculations easier and solve problems for missing values. The following table summarizes commonly used properties of real numbers.

Property	Addition	Multiplication
Commutative	$a + b = b + a$	$a \times b = b \times a$
Associative	$(a + b) + c = a + (b + c)$	$(a \times b) \times c = a \times (bc)$
Identity	$a + 0 = a; 0 + a = a$	$a \times 1 = a; 1 \times a = a$
Inverse	$a + (-a) = 0$	$a \times \dfrac{1}{a} = 1; a \neq 0$
Distributive	$a(b + c) = ab + ac$	

The cumulative property of addition states that the order in which numbers are added does not change the sum. Similarly, the commutative property of multiplication states that the order in which numbers are multiplied does not change the product. The associative property of addition and multiplication state that the grouping of numbers being added or multiplied does not change the sum or product, respectively. The commutative and associative properties are useful for performing calculations. For example, $(47 + 25) + 3$ is equivalent to $(47 + 3) + 25$, which is easier to calculate.

The identity property of addition states that adding zero to any number does not change its value. The identity property of multiplication states that multiplying a number by 1 does not change its value. The inverse property of addition states that the sum of a number and its opposite equals zero. Opposites are numbers that are the same with different signs (ex. 5 and -5; $-\frac{1}{2}$ and $\frac{1}{2}$). The inverse property of multiplication states that the product of a number (other than 0) and its reciprocal equals 1. Reciprocal numbers have numerators and denominators that are inverted (ex. $\frac{2}{5}$ and $\frac{5}{2}$). Inverse properties are useful for canceling quantities to find missing values (see algebra content). For example, $a + 7 = 12$ is solved by adding the inverse of 7(-7) to both sides in order to isolate a.

The distributive property states that multiplying a sum (or difference) by a number produces the same result as multiplying each value in the sum (or difference) by the number and adding (or subtracting) the products. Consider the following scenario: You are buying three tickets for a baseball game. Each ticket costs $18. You are also charged a fee of $2 per ticket for purchasing the tickets online. The cost is calculated: $3 \times 18 + 3 \times 2$. Using the distributive property, the cost can also be calculated $3(18 + 2)$.

Estimation

Estimation is finding a value that is close to a solution but is not the exact answer. For example, if there are values in the thousands to be multiplied, then each value can be estimated to the nearest thousand and the calculation performed. This value provides an approximate solution that can be determined very quickly.

Rounding is the process of either bumping a number up or down, based on a specified place value. First, the place value is specified. Then, the digit to its right is looked at. For example, if rounding to the nearest hundreds place, the digit in the tens place is used. If it is a 0, 1, 2, 3, or 4, the digit being rounded to is left alone. If it is a 5, 6, 7, 8 or 9, the digit being rounded to is increased by one. All other digits before the decimal point are then changed to zeros, and the digits in decimal places are dropped. If a decimal place is being rounded to, all subsequent digits are just dropped. For example, if 845,231.45 was to be rounded to the nearest thousands place, the answer would be 845,000. The 5 would remain the same due to the 2 in the hundreds place. Also, if 4.567 was to be rounded to the nearest tenths place, the answer would be 4.6. The 5 increased to 6 due to the 6 in the hundredths place, and the rest of the decimal is dropped.

Sometimes when performing operations such as multiplying numbers, the result can be estimated by *rounding*. For example, to estimate the value of 11.2×2.01, each number can be rounded to the nearest integer. This will yield a result of 22.

Rounding numbers helps with estimation because it changes the given number to a simpler, although less accurate, number than the exact given number. Rounding allows for easier calculations, which estimate the results of using the exact given number. The accuracy of the estimate and ease of use depends on the place value to which the number is rounded. Rounding numbers consists of:

- determining what place value the number is being rounded to
- examining the digit to the right of the desired place value to decide whether to round up or keep the digit, and
- replacing all digits to the right of the desired place value with zeros.

To round 746,311 to the nearest ten thousand, the digit in the ten thousands place should be located first. In this case, this digit is 4 (7<u>4</u>6,311). Then, the digit to its right is examined. If this digit is 5 or greater, the number will be rounded up by increasing the digit in the desired place by one. If the digit to the right of the place value being rounded is 4 or less, the number will be kept the same. For the given example, the digit being examined is a 6, which means that the number will be rounded up by increasing the digit to the left by one. Therefore, the digit 4 is changed to a 5. Finally, to write the rounded number, any digits to the left of the place value being rounded remain the same and any to its right are replaced with zeros. For the given example, rounding 746,311 to the nearest ten thousand will produce 750,000. To round 746,311 to the nearest hundred, the digit to the right of the three in the hundreds place is examined to determine whether to round up or keep the same number. In this case, that digit is a 1, so the number will be kept the same and any digits to its right will be replaced with zeros. The resulting rounded number is 746,300.

Rounding place values to the right of the decimal follows the same procedure, but digits being replaced by zeros can simply be dropped. To round 3.752891 to the nearest thousandth, the desired place value is located (3.752891) and the digit to the right is examined. In this case, the digit 8 indicates that the number will be rounded up, and the 2 in the thousandths place will increase to a 3. Rounding up and replacing the digits to the right of the thousandths place produces 3.753000 which is equivalent to 3.753. Therefore, the zeros are not necessary and the rounded number should be written as 3.753.

When rounding up, if the digit to be increased is a 9, the digit to its left is increased by 1 and the digit in the desired place value is changed to a zero. For example, the number 1,598 rounded to the nearest ten is 1,600. Another example shows the number 43.72961 rounded to the nearest thousandth is 43.730 or 43.73.

Mental math should always be considered as problems are worked through, and the ability to work through problems in one's head helps save time. If a problem is simple enough, such as $15 + 3 = 18$, it should be completed mentally. The ability to do this will increase once addition and subtraction in higher place values are grasped. Also, mental math is important in multiplication and division. The times tables multiplying all numbers from 1 to 12 should be memorized. This will allow for division within those numbers to be memorized as well. For example, we should know easily that $121 \div 11 = 11$ because it should be memorized that $11 \times 11 = 121$. Here is the multiplication table to be memorized:

x	1	2	3	4	5	6	7	8	9	10	11	12	13	14	15
1	1	2	3	4	5	6	7	8	9	10	11	12	13	14	15
2	2	4	6	8	10	12	14	16	18	20	22	24	26	28	30
3	3	6	9	12	15	18	21	24	27	30	33	36	39	42	45
4	4	8	12	16	20	24	28	32	36	40	44	48	52	56	60
5	5	10	15	20	25	30	35	40	45	50	55	60	65	70	75
6	6	12	18	24	30	36	42	48	54	60	66	72	78	84	90
7	7	14	21	28	35	42	49	56	63	70	77	84	91	98	105
8	8	16	24	32	40	48	56	64	72	80	88	96	104	112	120
9	9	18	27	36	45	54	63	72	81	90	99	108	117	126	135
10	10	20	30	40	50	60	70	80	90	100	110	120	130	140	150
11	11	22	33	44	55	66	77	88	99	110	121	132	143	154	165
12	12	24	36	48	60	72	84	96	108	120	132	144	156	168	180
13	13	26	39	52	65	78	91	104	117	130	143	156	169	182	195
14	14	28	42	56	70	84	98	112	126	140	154	168	182	196	210
15	15	30	45	60	75	90	105	120	135	150	165	180	195	210	225

The values in yellow along the diagonal of the table consist of *perfect squares*. A perfect square is a number that represents a product of two equal integers.

Rational Numbers

The mathematical number system is made up of two general types of numbers: real and complex. *Real numbers* are those that are used in normal settings, while *complex numbers* are those composed of both a real number and an imaginary one. Imaginary numbers are the result of taking the square root of -1, and $\sqrt{-1} = i$.

The real number system is often explained using a Venn diagram similar to the one below. After a number has been labeled as a real number, further classification occurs when considering the other groups in this diagram. If a number is a never-ending, non-repeating decimal, it falls in the irrational category. Otherwise, it is rational. More information on these types of numbers is given in the section above. Furthermore, if a number does not have a fractional part, it is classified as an integer, such as -2, 75, or 0. Whole numbers are an even smaller group that only includes positive integers and 0. The last group of natural numbers is made up of only positive integers, such as 2, 56, or 12.

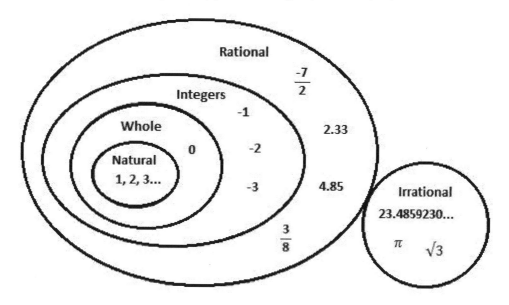

Real numbers can be compared and ordered using the number line. If a number falls to the left on the real number line, it is less than a number on the right. For example, $-2 < 5$ because -2 falls to the left of 0, and 5 falls to the right.

Complex numbers are made up of the sum of a real number and an imaginary number. Some examples of complex numbers include $6 + 2i$, $5 - 7i$, and $-3 + 12i$. Adding and subtracting complex numbers is similar to collecting like terms. The real numbers are added together, and the imaginary numbers are added together. For example, if the problem asks to simplify the given expression $6 + 2i - 3 + 7i$, the 6 and -3 would combine to make 3, and the $2i$ and $7i$ combine to make $9i$. Multiplying and dividing complex numbers is similar to working with exponents. One rule to remember when multiplying is that $i * i = -1$. For example, if a problem asks to simplify the expression $4i(3 + 7i)$, the $4i$ should be distributed throughout the 3 and the $7i$. This leaves the final expression $12i - 28$. The 28 is negative because $i * i$ results in a negative number. The last type of operation to consider with complex numbers is the conjugate. The *conjugate* of a complex number is a technique used to change the complex number into a real number. For example, the conjugate of $4 - 3i$ is $4 + 3i$. Multiplying $(4 - 3i)(4 + 3i)$ results in $16 + 12i - 12i + 9$, which has a final answer of $16 + 9 = 25$.

Integers are the whole numbers together with their negatives. They include numbers like 5, 24, 0, -6, and 15. They do not include fractions or numbers that have digits after the decimal point.

Rational numbers are all numbers that can be written as a fraction using integers. A *fraction* is written as $\frac{x}{y}$ and represents the quotient of x being divided by y. More practically, it means dividing the whole into y equal parts, then taking x of those parts.

Examples of rational numbers include $\frac{1}{2}$ and $\frac{5}{4}$. The number on the top is called the *numerator*, and the number on the bottom is called the *denominator*. Because every integer can be written as a fraction with a denominator of 1, (e.g. $\frac{3}{1} = 3$), every integer is also a rational number.

When adding integers and negative rational numbers, there are some basic rules to determine if the solution is negative or positive:

- Adding two positive numbers results in a positive value: $3.3 + 4.8 = 8.1$.
- Adding two negative numbers results in a negative number: $(-8) + (-6) = -14$.

Adding one positive and one negative number requires taking the absolute values and finding the difference between them. Then, the sign of the number that has the higher absolute value for the final solution is used.

For example, $(-9) + 11$, has a difference of absolute values of 2. The final solution is 2 because 11 has the higher absolute value. Another example is $9 + (-11)$, which has a difference of absolute values of 2. The final solution is -2 because 11 has the higher absolute value.

When subtracting integers and negative rational numbers, one has to change the problem to adding the opposite and then apply the rules of addition.

- Subtracting two positive numbers is the same as adding one positive and one negative number.
    - For example, $4.9 - 7.1$ is the same as $4.9 + (-7.1)$. The solution is -2.2 since the absolute value of -7.1 is greater. Another example is $8.5 - 6.4$ which is the same as $8.5 + (-6.4)$. The solution is 2.1 since the absolute value of 8.5 is greater.
- Subtracting a positive number from a negative number results in negative value.
    - For example, $(-12) - 7$ is the same as $(-12) + (-7)$ with a solution of -19.
- Subtracting a negative number from a positive number results in a positive value.
    - For example, $12 - (-7)$ is the same as $12 + 7$ with a solution of 19.
- For multiplication and division of integers and rational numbers, if both numbers are positive or both numbers are negative, the result is a positive value.
    - For example, $(-1.7)(-4)$ has a solution of 6.8 since both numbers are negative values.
- If one number is positive and another number is negative, the result is a negative value.
    - For example, $(-15)/5$ has a solution of -3 since there is one negative number.

As mentioned, rational numbers are any number which can be written as a fraction or ratio. Within the set of rational numbers, several subsets exist which are referenced throughout the mathematics topics. Counting numbers are the first numbers learned as a child. Counting numbers consist of 1,2,3,4, and so on. Whole numbers include all counting numbers and zero (0,1,2,3,4,...). Integers include counting numbers, their opposites, and zero (...,-3,-2,-1,0,1,2,3,...). Rational numbers are inclusive of integers, fractions, and decimals that terminate, or end (1.7, 0.04213) or repeat (0.136$\overline{5}$).

When comparing or ordering numbers, the numbers should be written in the same format (decimal or fraction), if possible. For example, $\sqrt{49}$, 7.3, and $\frac{15}{2}$ are easier to order if each one is converted to a decimal, such as 7, 7.3, and 7.5 (converting fractions and decimals is covered in the following section). A number line is used to order and compare the numbers. Any number that is to the right of another number is greater than that number. Conversely, a number positioned to the left of a given number is less than that number.

Sequences and Series

Patterns within a sequence can come in 2 distinct forms: the items (shapes, numbers, etc.) either repeat in a constant order, or the items change from one step to another in some consistent way. The core is the smallest unit, or number of items, that repeats in a repeating pattern. For example, the pattern oo▲oo▲o... has a core that is oo▲. Knowing only the core, the pattern can be extended. Knowing the number of steps in the core allows the identification of an item in each step without drawing/writing the entire pattern out. For example, suppose the tenth item in the previous pattern must be determined. Because the core consists of three items (oo▲), the core repeats in multiples of 3. In other words, steps 3, 6, 9, 12, etc. will be ▲ completing the core with the core starting over on the next step. For the above example, the 9th step will be ▲ and the 10th will be o.

The most common patterns in which each item changes from one step to the next are arithmetic and geometric sequences. An arithmetic sequence is one in which the items increase or decrease by a constant difference. In other words, the same thing is added or subtracted to each item or step to produce the next. To determine if a sequence is arithmetic, determine what must be added or subtracted to step one to produce step two. Then, check if the same thing is added/subtracted to step two to produce step three. The same thing must be added/subtracted to step three to produce step four, and so on. Consider the pattern 13, 10, 7, 4 . . . To get from step one (13) to step two (10) by adding or subtracting requires subtracting by 3. The next step is checking if subtracting 3 from step two (10) will produce step three (7), and subtracting 3 from step three (7) will produce step four (4). In this case, the pattern holds true. Therefore, this is an arithmetic sequence in which each step is produced by subtracting 3 from the previous step. To extend the sequence, 3 is subtracted from the last step to produce the next. The next three numbers in the sequence are 1, -2, -5.

A geometric sequence is one in which each step is produced by multiplying or dividing the previous step by the same number. To determine if a sequence is geometric, decide what step one must be multiplied or divided by to produce step two. Then check if multiplying or dividing step two by the same number produces step three, and so on. Consider the pattern 2, 8, 32, 128 . . . To get from step one (2) to step two (8) requires multiplication by 4. The next step determines if multiplying step two (8) by 4 produces step three (32), and multiplying step three (32) by 4 produces step four (128). In this case, the pattern holds true. Therefore, this is a geometric sequence in which each step is produced by multiplying the previous step by 4. To extend the sequence, the last step is multiplied by 4 and repeated. The next three numbers in the sequence are 512; 2,048; 8,192.

Although arithmetic and geometric sequences typically use numbers, these sequences can also be represented by shapes. For example, an arithmetic sequence could consist of shapes with three sides, four sides, and five sides (add one side to the previous step to produce the next). A geometric sequence could consist of eight blocks, four blocks, and two blocks (each step is produced by dividing the number of blocks in the previous step by 2).

Frequencies

In mathematics, frequencies refer to how often an event occurs or the number of times a particular quantity appears in a given series. To find the number of times a specific value appears, frequency tables are used to record the occurrences, which can then be summed. To construct a frequency table, one simply inputs the values into a tabular format with a column denoting each value, typically in ascending order, with a second column to tally up the number of occurrences for each value, and a third column to give a numerical frequency based on the number of tallies.

A *frequency distribution* communicates the number of outcomes of a given value or number in a data set. When displayed as a bar graph or histogram, it can visually indicate the spread and distribution of the data. A histogram resembling a bell curve approximates a normal distribution. A frequency distribution can also be displayed as a *stem-and-leaf plot*, which arranges data in numerical order and displays values similar to a tally chart with the stem being a range within the set and the leaf indicating the exact value. (Ex. stems are whole numbers and leaves are tenths.)

	Movie Ratings
4	7
5	2 6 9
6	1 4 6 8 8
7	0 3 5 9
8	1 3 5 6 8 8 9
9	0 0 1 3 4 6 6 9
Key	6 │ 1 represents 61

Stem	Leaf
2	0 2 3 6 8 8 9
3	2 6 7 7
4	7 9
5	4 6 9

This plot provides more detail about individual data points and allows for easy identification of the median, as well as any repeated values in the set.

Data that isn't described using numbers is known as *categorical data*. For example, age is numerical data but hair color is categorical data. Categorical data can also be summarized using two-way frequency tables. A *two-way frequency table* counts the relationship between two sets of categorical data. There are rows and columns for each category, and each cell represents frequency information that shows the actual data count between each combination. For example, below is a two-way frequency table showing the gender and breed of cats in an animal shelter:

	Domestic Shorthair	Persian	Domestic Longhair	Total
Male	12	2	7	21
Female	8	4	5	17
Total	20	6	12	38

Entries in the middle of the table are known as the *joint frequencies*. For example, the number of females that are Persians is 4, which is a joint frequency. The totals are the *marginal frequencies*. For example, the total number of males is 21, which is a marginal frequency. If the frequencies are changed into percentages based on totals, the table is known as a *two-way relative frequency table*. Percentages can be calculated using the table total, the row totals, or the column totals. Two-way frequency tables can help in making conclusions about the data.

Algebra

Algebraic Expressions and Equations

An algebraic expression is a statement about an unknown quantity expressed in mathematical symbols. A variable is used to represent the unknown quantity, usually denoted by a letter. An equation is a statement in which two expressions (at least one containing a variable) are equal to each other. An algebraic expression can be thought of as a mathematical phrase and an equation can be thought of as a mathematical sentence.

Algebraic expressions and equations both contain numbers, variables, and mathematical operations. The following are examples of algebraic expressions: $5x + 3, 7xy - 8(x^2 + y)$, and $\sqrt{a^2 + b^2}$. An expression can be simplified or evaluated for given values of variables. The following are examples of equations: $2x + 3 = 7, a^2 + b^2 = c^2$, and $2x + 5 = 3x - 2$. An equation contains two sides separated by an equal sign. Equations can be solved to determine the value(s) of the variable for which the statement is true.

Adding and Subtracting Linear Algebraic Expressions

An algebraic expression is simplified by combining like terms. A term is a number, variable, or product of a number, and variables separated by addition and subtraction. For the algebraic expression $3x^2 - 4x + 5 - 5x^2 + x - 3$, the terms are $3x^2$, -4x, 5, -5x², x, and -3. Like terms have the same variables raised to the same powers (exponents). The like terms for the previous example are $3x^2$ and -5x², -4x and x, 5 and -3. To combine like terms, the coefficients (numerical factor of the term including sign) are added and the variables and their powers are kept the same. Note that if a coefficient is not written, it is an implied coefficient of 1 ($x = 1x$). The previous example will simplify to $-2x^2 - 3x + 2$.

When adding or subtracting algebraic expressions, each expression is written in parenthesis. The negative sign is distributed when necessary, and like terms are combined. Consider the following: add

$2a + 5b - 2$ to $a - 2b + 8c - 4$. The sum is set as follows: $(a - 2b + 8c - 4) + (2a + 5b - 2)$. In front of each set of parenthesis is an implied positive one, which, when distributed, does not change any of the terms. Therefore, the parentheses are dropped and like terms are combined: $a - 2b + 8c - 4 + 2a + 5b - 2 = 3a + 3b + 8c - 6$.

Consider the following problem: Subtract $2a + 5b - 2$ from $a - 2b + 8c - 4$. The difference is set as follows: $(a - 2b + 8c - 4) - (2a + 5b - 2)$. The implied one in front of the first set of parenthesis will not change those four terms. However, distributing the implied -1 in front of the second set of parenthesis will change the sign of each of those three terms: $a - 2b + 8c - 4 - 2a - 5b + 2$. Combining like terms yields the simplified expression $-a - 7b + 8c - 2$.

Distributive Property

The distributive property states that multiplying a sum (or difference) by a number produces the same result as multiplying each value in the sum (or difference) by the number and adding (or subtracting) the products. Using mathematical symbols, the distributive property states $a(b + c) = ab + ac$. The expression $4(3 + 2)$ is simplified using the order of operations. Simplifying inside the parenthesis first produces 4×5, which equals 20. The expression $4(3 + 2)$ can also be simplified using the distributive property: $4(3 + 2) = 4 \times 3 + 4 \times 2 = 12 + 8 = 20$.

Consider the following example: $4(3x - 2)$. The expression cannot be simplified inside the parenthesis because $3x$ and -2 are not like terms, and therefore cannot be combined. However, the expression can be simplified by using the distributive property and multiplying each term inside of the parenthesis by the term outside of the parenthesis: $12x - 8$. The resulting equivalent expression contains no like terms, so it cannot be further simplified.

Consider the expression $(3x + 2y + 1) - (5x - 3) + 2(3y + 4)$. Again, there are no like terms, but the distributive property is used to simplify the expression. Note there is an implied one in front of the first set of parentheses and an implied -1 in front of the second set of parentheses. Distributing the one, -1, and 2 produces $1(3x) + 1(2y) + 1(1) - 1(5x) - 1(-3) + 2(3y) + 2(4) = 3x + 2y + 1 - 5x + 3 + 6y + 8$. This expression contains like terms that are combined to produce the simplified expression $-2x + 8y + 12$.

Algebraic expressions are tested to be equivalent by choosing values for the variables and evaluating both expressions (see 2.A.4). For example, $4(3x - 2)$ and $12x - 8$ are tested by substituting 3 for the variable x and calculating to determine if equivalent values result.

Simple Expressions for Given Values

An algebraic expression is a statement written in mathematical symbols, typically including one or more unknown values represented by variables. For example, the expression $2x + 3$ states that an unknown number (x) is multiplied by 2 and added to 3. If given a value for the unknown number, or variable, the value of the expression is determined. For example, if the value of the variable x is 4, the value of the expression 4 is multiplied by 2, and 3 is added. This results in a value of 11 for the expression.

When given an algebraic expression and values for the variable(s), the expression is evaluated to determine its numerical value. To evaluate the expression, the given values for the variables are substituted (or replaced) and the expression is simplified using the order of operations. Parenthesis should be used when substituting. Consider the following: Evaluate $a - 2b + ab$ for $a = 3$ and $b = -1$.

30

To evaluate, any variable a is replaced with 3 and any variable b with -1, producing (3)-2(-1)+(3)(-1). Next, the order of operations is used to calculate the value of the expression, which is 2.

Parts of Expressions

Algebraic expressions consist of variables, numbers, and operations. A term of an expression is any combination of numbers and/or variables, and terms are separated by addition and subtraction. For example, the expression $5x^2 - 3xy + 4 - 2$ consists of 4 terms: $5x^2$, -3xy, 4y, and -2. Note that each term includes its given sign (+ or −). The variable part of a term is a letter that represents an unknown quantity. The coefficient of a term is the number by which the variable is multiplied. For the term 4y, the variable is y and the coefficient is 4. Terms are identified by the power (or exponent) of its variable.

A number without a variable is referred to as a constant. If the variable is to the first power (x^1 or simply x), it is referred to as a linear term. A term with a variable to the second power (x^2) is quadratic and a term to the third power (x^3) is cubic. Consider the expression $x^3 + 3x - 1$. The constant is -1. The linear term is 3x. There is no quadratic term. The cubic term is x^3.

An algebraic expression can also be classified by how many terms exist in the expression. Any like terms should be combined before classifying. A monomial is an expression consisting of only one term. Examples of monomials are: 17, 2x, and $-5ab^2$. A binomial is an expression consisting of two terms separated by addition or subtraction. Examples include $2x - 4$ and $-3y^2 + 2y$. A trinomial consists of 3 terms. For example, $5x^2 - 2x + 1$ is a trinomial.

Verbal Statements and Algebraic Expressions

An algebraic expression is a statement about unknown quantities expressed in mathematical symbols. The statement *five times a number added to forty* is expressed as $5x + 40$. An equation is a statement in which two expressions (with at least one containing a variable) are equal to one another. The statement *five times a number added to forty is equal to ten* is expressed as $5x + 40 = 10$.

Real world scenarios can also be expressed mathematically. Suppose a job pays its employees $300 per week and $40 for each sale made. The weekly pay is represented by the expression $40x + 300$ where x is the number of sales made during the week.

Consider the following scenario: Bob had $20 and Tom had $4. After selling 4 ice cream cones to Bob, Tom has as much money as Bob. The cost of an ice cream cone is an unknown quantity and can be represented by a variable (x). The amount of money Bob has after his purchase is four times the cost of an ice cream cone subtracted from his original $20 $\rightarrow 20 - 4x$. The amount of money Tom has after his sale is four times the cost of an ice cream cone added to his original $4 $\rightarrow 4x + 4$. After the sale, the amount of money that Bob and Tom have are equal $\rightarrow 20 - 4x = 4x + 4$.

When expressing a verbal or written statement mathematically, it is vital to understand words or phrases that can be represented with symbols. The following are examples:

Symbol	Phrase
+	Added to; increased by; sum of; more than
−	Decreased by; difference between; less than; take away
×	Multiplied by; 3(4,5...) times as large; product of
÷	Divided by; quotient of; half (third, etc.) of
=	Is; the same as; results in; as much as; equal to
x,t,n, etc.	A number; unknown quantity; value of; variable

Use of Formulas

Formulas are mathematical expressions that define the value of one quantity, given the value of one or more different quantities. Formulas look like equations because they contain variables, numbers, operators, and an equal sign. All formulas are equations but not all equations are formulas. A formula must have more than one variable. For example, $2x + 7 = y$ is an equation and a formula (it relates the unknown quantities x and y). However, $2x + 7 = 3$ is an equation but not a formula (it only expresses the value of the unknown quantity x).

Formulas are typically written with one variable alone (or isolated) on one side of the equal sign. This variable can be thought of as the *subject* in that the formula is stating the value of the *subject* in terms of the relationship between the other variables. Consider the distance formula: $distance = rate \times time$ or $d = rt$. The value of the subject variable d (distance) is the product of the variable r and t (rate and time). Given the rate and time, the distance traveled can easily be determined by substituting the values into the formula and evaluating.

The formula $P = 2l + 2w$ expresses how to calculate the perimeter of a rectangle (P) given its length (l) and width (w). To find the perimeter of a rectangle with a length of 3ft and a width of 2ft, these values are substituted into the formula for l and w: $P = 2(3ft) + 2(2ft)$. Following the order of operations, the perimeter is determined to be 10ft. When working with formulas such as these, including units is an important step.

Given a formula expressed in terms of one variable, the formula can be manipulated to express the relationship in terms of any other variable. In other words, the formula can be rearranged to change which variable is the *subject*. To solve for a variable of interest by manipulating a formula, the equation may be solved as if all other variables were numbers. The same steps for solving are followed, leaving operations in terms of the variables instead of calculating numerical values. For the formula $P = 2l + 2w$, the perimeter is the subject expressed in terms of the length and width. To write a formula to calculate the width of a rectangle, given its length and perimeter, the previous formula relating the three variables is solved for the variable w. If P and l were numerical values, this is a two-step linear equation solved by subtraction and division. To solve the equation $P = 2l + 2w$ for w, $2l$ is first subtracted from both sides: $P - 2l = 2w$. Then both sides are divided by 2: $\frac{P-2l}{2} = w$.

Dependent and Independent Variables

A variable represents an unknown quantity and, in the case of a formula, a specific relationship exists between the variables. Within a given scenario, variables are the quantities that are changing. If two variables exist, one is dependent and one is independent. The value of one variable depends on the other variable. If a scenario describes distance traveled and time traveled at a given speed, distance is dependent and time is independent. The distance traveled depends on the time spent traveling. If a scenario describes the cost of a cab ride and the distance traveled, the cost is dependent and the distance is independent. The cost of a cab ride depends on the distance travelled. Formulas often contain more than two variables and are typically written with the dependent variable alone on one side of the equation. This lone variable is the *subject* of the statement. If a formula contains three or more variables, one variable is dependent and the rest are independent. The values of all independent variables are needed to determine the value of the dependent variable.

The formula $P = 2l + 2w$ expresses the dependent variable P in terms of the independent variables, l and w. The perimeter of a rectangle depends on its length and width. The formula $d = rt$ ($distance = rate \times time$) expresses the dependent variable d in terms of the independent variables, r and t. The distance traveled depends on the rate (or speed) and the time traveled.

Multistep One-Variable Linear Equations and Inequalities

Linear equations and linear inequalities are both comparisons of two algebraic expressions. However, unlike equations in which the expressions are equal, linear inequalities compare expressions that may be unequal. Linear equations typically have one value for the variable that makes the statement true. Linear inequalities generally have an infinite number of values that make the statement true.

When solving a linear equation, the desired result requires determining a numerical value for the unknown variable. If given a linear equation involving addition, subtraction, multiplication, or division, working backwards isolates the variable. Addition and subtraction are inverse operations, as are multiplication and division. Therefore, they can be used to cancel each other out.

The first steps to solving linear equations are distributing, if necessary, and combining any like terms on the same side of the equation. Sides of an equation are separated by an *equal* sign. Next, the equation is manipulated to show the variable on one side. Whatever is done to one side of the equation must be done to the other side of the equation to remain equal. Inverse operations are then used to isolate the variable and undo the order of operations backwards. Addition and subtraction are undone, then multiplication and division are undone.

For example, solve $4(t - 2) + 2t - 4 = 2(9 - 2t)$

Distributing: $4t - 8 + 2t - 4 = 18 - 4t$

Combining like terms: $6t - 12 = 18 - 4t$

Adding $4t$ to each side to move the variable: $10t - 12 = 18$

Adding 12 to each side to isolate the variable: $10t = 30$

Dividing each side by 10 to isolate the variable: $t = 3$

The answer can be checked by substituting the value for the variable into the original equation, ensuring that both sides calculate to be equal.

Linear inequalities express the relationship between unequal values. More specifically, they describe in what way the values are unequal. A value can be greater than (>), less than (<), greater than or equal to (≥), or less than or equal to (≤) another value. $5x + 40 > 65$ is read as *five times a number added to forty is greater than sixty-five.*

When solving a linear inequality, the solution is the set of all numbers that make the statement true. The inequality $x + 2 \geq 6$ has a solution set of 4 and every number greater than 4 (4.01; 5; 12; 107; etc.). Adding 2 to 4 or any number greater than 4 results in a value that is greater than or equal to 6. Therefore, $x \geq 4$ is the solution set.

To algebraically solve a linear inequality, follow the same steps as those for solving a linear equation. The inequality symbol stays the same for all operations *except* when multiplying or dividing by a negative number. If multiplying or dividing by a negative number while solving an inequality, the relationship reverses (the sign flips). In other words, > switches to < and vice versa. Multiplying or dividing by a positive number does not change the relationship, so the sign stays the same. An example is shown below.

Solve $-2x - 8 \leq 22$

Add 8 to both sides: $-2x \leq 30$

Divide both sides by -2: $x \geq -15$

Solutions of a linear equation or a linear inequality are the values of the variable that make a statement true. In the case of a linear equation, the solution set (list of all possible solutions) typically consists of a single numerical value. To find the solution, the equation is solved by isolating the variable. For example, solving the equation $3x - 7 = -13$ produces the solution $x = -2$. The only value for x which produces a true statement is -2. This can be checked by substituting -2 into the original equation to check that both sides are equal. In this case, $3(-2) - 7 = -13 \rightarrow -13 = -13$; therefore, -2 is a solution.

Although linear equations generally have one solution, this is not always the case. If there is no value for the variable that makes the statement true, there is no solution to the equation. Consider the equation $x + 3 = x - 1$. There is no value for x in which adding 3 to the value produces the same result as subtracting one from the value. Conversely, if any value for the variable makes a true statement, the equation has an infinite number of solutions. Consider the equation $3x + 6 = 3(x + 2)$. Any number substituted for x will result in a true statement (both sides of the equation are equal).

By manipulating equations like the two above, the variable of the equation will cancel out completely. If the remaining constants express a true statement (ex. $6 = 6$), then all real numbers are solutions to the equation. If the constants left express a false statement (ex. $3 = -1$), then no solution exists for the equation.

Solving a linear inequality requires all values that make the statement true to be determined. For example, solving $3x - 7 \geq -13$ produces the solution $x \geq -2$. This means that -2 and any number greater than -2 produces a true statement. Solution sets for linear inequalities will often be displayed using a number line. If a value is included in the set ($\geq$ or $\leq$), a shaded dot is placed on that value and an arrow extending in the direction of the solutions. For a variable > or $\geq$ a number, the arrow will point right on a number line, the direction where the numbers increase. If a variable is < or $\leq$ a number, the arrow will point left on a number line, which is the direction where the numbers decrease. If the value is not included in the set (> or <), an open (unshaded) circle on that value is used with an arrow in the appropriate direction.

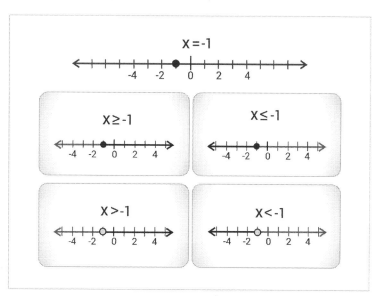

Similar to linear equations, a linear inequality may have a solution set consisting of all real numbers, or can contain no solution. When solved algebraically, a linear inequality in which the variable cancels out and results in a true statement (ex. $7 \geq 2$) has a solution set of all real numbers. A linear inequality in which the variable cancels out and results in a false statement (ex. $7 \leq 2$) has no solution.

Linear Relationships

Linear relationships describe the way two quantities change with respect to each other. The relationship is defined as linear because a line is produced if all the sets of corresponding values are graphed on a coordinate grid. When expressing the linear relationship as an equation, the equation is often written in the form $y = mx + b$ (slope-intercept form) where m and b are numerical values and x and y are variables (for example, $y = 5x + 10$). Given a linear equation and the value of either variable (x or y), the value of the other variable can be determined.

Suppose a teacher is grading a test containing 20 questions with 5 points given for each correct answer, adding a curve of 10 points to each test. This linear relationship can be expressed as the equation $y = 5x + 10$ where x represents the number of correct answers and y represents the test score. To determine the score of a test with a given number of correct answers, the number of correct answers is substituted into the equation for x and evaluated. For example, for 10 correct answers, 10 is substituted for x: $y = 5(10) + 10 \rightarrow y = 60$. Therefore, 10 correct answers will result in a score of 60. The number of correct answers needed to obtain a certain score can also be determined. To determine the number of correct answers needed to score a 90, 90 is substituted for y in the equation (y represents the test score) and solved: $90 = 5x + 10 \rightarrow 80 = 5x \rightarrow 16 = x$. Therefore, 16 correct answers are needed to score a 90.

Linear relationships may be represented by a table of 2 corresponding values. Certain tables may determine the relationship between the values and predict other corresponding sets. Consider the table below, which displays the money in a checking account that charges a monthly fee:

Month	0	1	2	3	4
Balance	$210	$195	$180	$165	$150

An examination of the values reveals that the account loses $15 every month (the month increases by one and the balance decreases by 15). This information can be used to predict future values. To determine what the value will be in month 6, the pattern can be continued, and it can be concluded that the balance will be $120. To determine which month the balance will be $0, $210 is divided by $15 (since the balance decreases $15 every month), resulting in month 14.

Similar to a table, a graph can display corresponding values of a linear relationship.

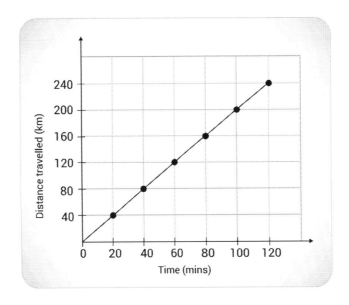

The graph above represents the relationship between distance traveled and time. To find the distance traveled in 80 minutes, the mark for 80 minutes is located at the bottom of the graph. By following this mark directly up on the graph, the corresponding point for 80 minutes is directly across from the 160 kilometer mark. This information indicates that the distance travelled in 80 minutes is 160 kilometers. To predict information not displayed on the graph, the way in which the variables change with respect to one another is determined. In this case, distance increases by 40 kilometers as time increases by 20 minutes. This information can be used to continue the data in the graph or convert the values to a table.

Conjectures, Predictions, or Generalizations Based on Patterns

An arithmetic or geometric sequence can be written as a formula and used to determine unknown steps without writing out the entire sequence. (Note that a similar process for repeating patterns is covered in the previous section.) An arithmetic sequence progresses by a *common difference*. To determine the common difference, any step is subtracted by the step that precedes it. In the sequence 4, 9, 14, 19 . . .

the common difference, or d, is 5. By expressing each step as a_1, a_2, a_3, etc., a formula can be written to represent the sequence. a_1 is the first step. To produce step two, step 1 (a_1) is added to the common difference (d): $a_2 = a_1 + d$. To produce step three, the common difference (d) is added twice to a_1: $a_3 = a_1 + 2d$. To produce step four, the common difference (d) is added three times to a_1: $a_4 = a_1 + 3d$. Following this pattern allows a general rule for arithmetic sequences to be written. For any term of the sequence (a_n), the first step (a_1) is added to the product of the common difference (d) and one less than the step of the term ($n - 1$): $a_n = a_1 + (n - 1)d$. Suppose the 8th term (a_8) is to be found in the previous sequence. By knowing the first step (a_1) is 4 and the common difference (d) is 5, the formula can be used: $a_n = a_1 + (n - 1)d \rightarrow a_8 = 4 + (7)5 \rightarrow a_8 = 39$.

In a geometric sequence, each step is produced by multiplying or dividing the previous step by the same number. The *common ratio*, or (r), can be determined by dividing any step by the previous step. In the sequence 1, 3, 9, 27 . . . the common ratio (r) is 3($\frac{3}{1} = 3$ or $\frac{9}{3} = 3$ or $\frac{27}{9} = 3$). Each successive step can be expressed as a product of the first step (a_1) and the common ratio (r) to some power. For example, $a_2 = a_1 \times r; a_3 = a_1 \times r \times r$ or $a_3 = a_1 \times r^2; a_4 = a_1 \times r \times r \times r$ or $a_4 = a\_1 \times r^3$. Following this pattern, a general rule for geometric sequences can be written. For any term of the sequence (a_n), the first step (a_1) is multiplied by the common ratio (r) raised to the power one less than the step of the term ($n - 1$): $a_n = a_1 \times r^{(n-1)}$. Suppose for the previous sequence, the 7th term (a_7) is to be found. Knowing the first step (a_1) is one, and the common ratio (r) is 3, the formula can be used: $a_n = a_1 \times r^{(n-1)} \rightarrow a_7 = (1) \times 3^6 \rightarrow a_7 = 729$.

Corresponding Terms of Two Numerical Patterns

When given two numerical patterns, the corresponding terms should be examined to determine if a relationship exists between them. Corresponding terms between patterns are the pairs of numbers that appear in the same step of the two sequences. Consider the following patterns 1, 2, 3, 4 . . . and 3, 6, 9, 12 . . . The corresponding terms are: 1 and 3; 2 and 6; 3 and 9; and 4 and 12. To identify the relationship, each pair of corresponding terms is examined and the possibilities of performing an operation (+, −, ×, ÷) to the term from the first sequence to produce the corresponding term in the second sequence are determined. In this case:

$1 + 2 = 3$	or	$1 \times 3 = 3$	
$2 + 4 = 6$	or	$2 \times 3 = 6$	
$3 + 6 = 9$	or	$3 \times 3 = 9$	
$4 + 8 = 12$	or	$4 \times 3 = 12$	

The consistent pattern is that the number from the first sequence multiplied by 3 equals its corresponding term in the second sequence. By assigning each sequence a label (input and output) or variable (x and y), the relationship can be written as an equation. If the first sequence represents the inputs, or x, and the second sequence represents the outputs, or y, the relationship can be expressed as: $y = 3x$.

Consider the following sets of numbers:

a	2	4	6	8
b	6	8	10	12

To write a rule for the relationship between the values for *a* and the values for *b*, the corresponding terms (2 and 6; 4 and 8; 6 and 10; 8 and 12) are examined. The possibilities for producing *b* from *a* are:

$$2 + 4 = 6 \qquad \text{or} \qquad 2 \times 3 = 6$$

$$4 + 4 = 8 \qquad \text{or} \qquad 4 \times 2 = 8$$

$$6 + 4 = 10$$

$$8 + 4 = 12 \qquad \text{or} \qquad 8 \times 1.5 = 12$$

The consistent pattern is that adding 4 to the value of *a* produces the value of *b*. The relationship can be written as the equation $a + 4 = b$.

Geometry/Measurement

Geometry is part of mathematics. It deals with shapes and their properties. Geometry means knowing the names and properties of shapes. It is also similar to measurement and number operations. The basis of geometry involves being able to label and describe shapes and their properties. That knowledge will lead to working with formulas such as area, perimeter, and volume. This knowledge will help to solve word problems involving shapes.

Flat or two-dimensional shapes include circles, triangles, hexagons, and rectangles, among others. Three-dimensional solid shapes, such as spheres and cubes, are also used in geometry. A shape can be classified based on whether it is open like the letter U or closed like the letter O. Further classifications involve counting the number of sides and vertices (corners) on the shapes. This will help you tell the difference between shapes.

Polygons can be drawn by sketching a fixed number of line segments that meet to create a closed shape. In addition, *triangles* can be drawn by sketching a closed space using only three-line segments. *Quadrilaterals* are closed shapes with four-line segments. Note that a triangle has three vertices, and a quadrilateral has four vertices.

To draw circles, one curved line segment must be drawn that has only one endpoint. This creates a closed shape. Given such direction, every point on the line would be the same distance away from its center. The radius of a circle goes from an endpoint on the center of the circle to an endpoint on the circle. The diameter is the line segment created by placing an endpoint on the circle, drawing through the radius, and placing the other endpoint on the circle. A compass can be used to draw circles of a more precise size and shape.

Area and Perimeter
Area relates to two-dimensional geometric shapes. Basically, a figure is divided into two-dimensional units. The number of units needed to cover the figure is counted. Area is measured using square units, such as square inches, feet, centimeters, or kilometers.

Perimeter is the length of all its sides. The perimeter of a given closed sided figure would be found by first measuring the length of each side and then calculating the sum of all sides.

Formulas can be used to calculate area and perimeter. The area of a rectangle is found by multiplying its length, l, times its width, w. Therefore, the formula for area is $A = l \times w$. An equivalent expression is found by using the term base, b, instead of length, to represent the horizontal side of the shape. In this case, the formula is $A = b \times h$. This same formula can be used for all parallelograms. Here is a visualization of a rectangle with its labeled sides:

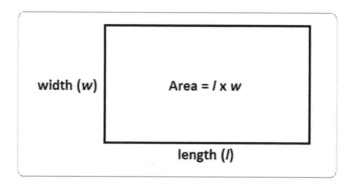

width (w)

Area = l x w

length (l)

A square has four equal sides with the length s. Its length is equal to its width. The formula for the area of a square is $A = s \times s$. Finally, the area of a triangle is calculated by dividing the area of the rectangle that would be formed by the base, the altitude, and height of the triangle. Therefore, the area of a triangle is $A = \frac{1}{2} \times b \times h$. Formulas for perimeter are derived by adding length measurements of the sides of a figure. The perimeter of a rectangle is the result of adding the length of the four sides. Therefore, the formula for perimeter of a rectangle is $P = 2 \times l + 2 \times w$, and the formula for perimeter of a square is $P = 4 \times s$. The perimeter of a triangle would be the sum of the lengths of the three sides.

Volume

Volume is a measurement of the amount of space that in a 3-dimensional figure. Volume is measured using cubic units, such as cubic inches, feet, centimeters, or kilometers.

Say you have 10 playing die that are each one cubic centimeter. Say you placed these along the length of a rectangle. Then 8 die are placed along its width. The remaining area is filled in with die. There would be 80 die in total. This would equal a volume of 80 cubic centimeters. Say the shape is doubled so that its height consists of two cube lengths. There would be 160 cubes. Also, its volume would be 160 cubic centimeters. Adding another level of cubes would mean that there would be $3 \times 80 = 240$ cubes. This idea shows that volume is calculated by multiplying area times height. The actual formula for volume of a three-dimensional rectangular solid is $V = l \times w \times h$. In this formula l represents length, w represents width, and h represents height. Volume can also be thought of as area of the base times the height. The base in this case would be the entire rectangle formed by l and w.

$A = L \times W \times H$

Here is an example of a rectangular solid with labeled sides:

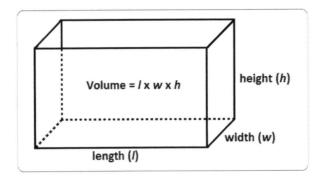

Volume = *l* x *w* x *h*

height (*h*)

width (*w*)

length (*l*)

A *cube* is a special type of rectangular solid in which its length, width, and height are the same. If this length is *s*, then the formula for the volume of a cube is $V = s \times s \times s$.

<u>Lines and Angles</u>

In geometry, a *line* connects two points, has no thickness, and extends indefinitely in both directions beyond the points. If it does end at two points, it is known as a *line segment*. It is important to distinguish between a line and a line segment.

An angle can be visualized as a corner. It is defined as the formation of two rays connecting at a vertex that extend indefinitely. Angles are measured in degrees. Their measurement is a measure of rotation. A full rotation equals 360 degrees and represents a circle. Half of a rotation equals 180 degrees and represents a half-circle. Subsequently, 90 degrees represents a quarter-circle. Similar to the hands on a clock, an angle begins at the center point, and two lines extend indefinitely from that point in two different directions.

A clock can be useful when learning how to measure angles. At 3:00, the big hand is on the 12 and the small hand is on the 3. The angle formed is 90 degrees and is known as a *right angle*. Any angle less than 90 degrees, such as the one formed at 2:00, is known as an *acute angle*. Any angle greater than 90 degrees is known as an *obtuse angle*. The entire clock represents 360 degrees, and each clockwise increment on the clock represents an addition of 30 degrees. Therefore, 6:00 represents 180 degrees, 7:00 represents 210 degrees, etc. Angle measurement is additive. An angle can be broken into two non-overlapping angles. The total measure of the larger angle is equal to the sum of the measurements of the two smaller angles.

A *ray* is a straight path that has an endpoint on one end and extends indefinitely in the other direction. Lines are known as being *coplanar* if they are located in the same plane. Coplanar lines exist within the same two-dimensional surface. Two lines are *parallel* if they are coplanar, extend in the same direction, and never cross. They are known as being *equidistant* because they are always the same distance from each other. If lines do cross, they are known as *intersecting lines*. As discussed previously, angles are utilized throughout geometry, and their measurement can be seen through the use of an analog clock. An angle is formed when two rays begin at the same endpoint. *Adjacent angles* can be formed by forming two angles out of one shared ray. They are two side-by-side angles that also share an endpoint.

Perpendicular lines are coplanar lines that form a right angle at their point of intersection. A triangle that contains a right angle is known as a *right triangle*. The sum of the angles within any triangle is always 180 degrees. Therefore, in a right triangle, the sum of the two angles that are not right angles is 90 degrees. Any two angles that sum up to 90 degrees are known as *complementary angles*. A triangle that contains an obtuse angle is known as an *obtuse triangle*. A triangle that contains three acute angles is known as an *acute triangle*. Here is an example of a 180-degree angle, split up into an acute and obtuse angle:

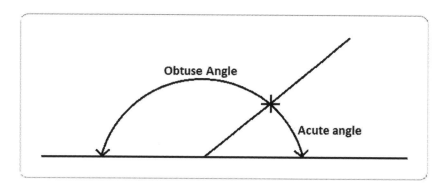

The vocabulary regarding many two-dimensional shapes is important to understand and use appropriately. Many four-sided figures can be identified using properties of angles and lines. A *quadrilateral* is a closed shape with four sides. A *parallelogram* is a specific type of quadrilateral that has two sets of parallel lines having the same length. A *trapezoid* is a quadrilateral having only one set of parallel sides. A *rectangle* is a parallelogram that has four right angles. A *rhombus* is a parallelogram with two acute angles, two obtuse angles, and four equal sides. The acute angles are of equal measure, and the obtuse angles are of equal measure. Finally, a *square* is a rhombus consisting of four right angles. It is important to note that some of these shapes share common attributes. For instance, all four-sided shapes are quadrilaterals. All squares are rectangles, but not all rectangles are squares.

Symmetry is another concept in geometry. If a two-dimensional shape can be folded along a straight line and the halves line up exactly, the figure is *symmetric*. The line is known as a *line of symmetry*. Circles, squares, and rectangles are examples of symmetric shapes.

Measuring Lengths of Objects

The length of an object can be measured using standard tools such as rulers, yard sticks, meter sticks, and measuring tapes. The following image depicts a yardstick:

Choosing the right tool to perform the measurement requires determining whether United States customary units or metric units are desired, and having a grasp of the approximate length of each unit and the approximate length of each tool. The measurement can still be performed by trial and error without the knowledge of the approximate size of the tool.

For example, to determine the length of a room in feet, a United States customary unit, various tools can be used for this task. These include a ruler (typically 12 inches/1 foot long), a yardstick (3 feet/1 yard long), or a tape measure displaying feet (typically either 25 feet or 50 feet). Because the length of a room is much larger than the length of a ruler or a yardstick, a tape measure should be used to perform the measurement.

When the correct measuring tool is selected, the measurement is performed by first placing the tool directly above or below the object (if making a horizontal measurement) or directly next to the object (if making a vertical measurement). The next step is aligning the tool so that one end of the object is at the mark for zero units, then recording the unit of the mark at the other end of the object. To give the length of a paperclip in metric units, a ruler displaying centimeters is aligned with one end of the paper clip to the mark for zero centimeters.

Directly down from the other end of the paperclip is the mark that measures its length. In this case, that mark is two small dashes past the 3 centimeter mark. Each small dash is 1 millimeter (or .1 centimeters). Therefore, the length of the paper clip is 3.2 centimeters.

To compare the lengths of objects, each length must be expressed in the same unit. If possible, the objects should be measured with the same tool or with tools utilizing the same units. For example, a ruler and a yardstick can both measure length in inches. If the lengths of the objects are expressed in different units, these different units must be converted to the same unit before comparing them. If two lengths are expressed in the same unit, the lengths may be compared by subtracting the smaller value from the larger value. For example, suppose the lengths of two gardens are to be compared. Garden A has a length of 4 feet, and garden B has a length of 2 yards. 2 yards is converted to 6 feet so that the measurements have similar units. Then, the smaller length (4 feet) is subtracted from the larger length (6ft): 6ft – 4ft = 2ft. Therefore, garden B is 2 feet larger than garden A.

Relative Sizes of United States Customary Units and Metric Units

The United States customary system and the metric system each consist of distinct units to measure lengths and volume of liquids. The U.S. customary units for length, from smallest to largest, are: inch (in), foot (ft), yard (yd), and mile (mi). The metric units for length, from smallest to largest, are: millimeter (mm), centimeter (cm), decimeter (dm), meter (m), and kilometer (km). The relative size of each unit of length is shown below.

U.S. Customary	Metric	Conversion
12in = 1ft	10mm = 1cm	1in = 254cm
36in = 3ft = 1yd	10cm = 1dm(decimeter)	1m ≈ 3.28ft ≈ 1.09yd
5,280ft = 1,760yd = 1mi	100cm = 10dm = 1m	1mi ≈ 1.6km
	1000m = 1km	

The U.S. customary units for volume of liquids, from smallest to largest, are: fluid ounces (fl oz), cup (c), pint (pt), quart (qt), and gallon (gal). The metric units for volume of liquids, from smallest to largest, are:

milliliter (mL), centiliter (cL), deciliter (dL), liter (L), and kiloliter (kL). The relative size of each unit of liquid volume is shown below.

U.S. Customary	Metric	Conversion
8fl oz = 1c	10mL = 1cL	1pt ≈ 0.473L
2c = 1pt	10cL = 1dL	1L ≈ 1.057qt
4c = 2pt = 1qt	1,000mL = 100cL = 10dL = 1L	1gal ≈ 3,785L
4qt = 1gal	1,000L = 1kL	

The U.S. customary system measures weight (how strongly Earth is pulling on an object) in the following units, from least to greatest: ounce (oz), pound (lb), and ton. The metric system measures mass (the quantity of matter within an object) in the following units, from least to greatest: milligram (mg), centigram (cg), gram (g), kilogram (kg), and metric ton (MT). The relative sizes of each unit of weight and mass are shown below.

U.S. Measures of Weight	Metric Measures of Mass
16oz = 1lb	10mg = 1cg
2,000lb = 1 ton	100cg = 1g
	1,000g = 1kg
	1,000kg = 1MT

Note that weight and mass DO NOT measure the same thing.

Time is measured in the following units, from shortest to longest: second (sec), minute (min), hour (h), day (d), week (wk), month (mo), year (yr), decade, century, millennium. The relative sizes of each unit of time is shown below.

- 60sec = 1min
- 60min = 1h
- 24hr = 1d
- 7d = 1wk
- 52wk = 1yr
- 12mo = 1yr
- 10yr = 1 decade
- 100yrs = 1 century
- 1,000yrs = 1 millennium

Conversion of Units

When working with different systems of measurement, conversion from one unit to another may be necessary. The conversion rate must be known to convert units. One method for converting units is to write and solve a proportion. The arrangement of values in a proportion is extremely important. Suppose that a problem requires converting 20 fluid ounces to cups. To do so, a proportion can be written using the conversion rate of 8fl oz = 1c with *x* representing the missing value. The proportion can be written in any of the following ways:

$$\frac{1}{8} = \frac{x}{20} \left(\frac{c\ for\ conversion}{fl\ oz\ for\ conversion} = \frac{unknown\ c}{fl\ oz\ given}\right); \frac{8}{1} = \frac{20}{x} \left(\frac{fl\ oz\ for\ conversion}{c\ for\ conversion} = \frac{fl\ oz\ given}{unknown\ c}\right);$$

$$\frac{1}{x} = \frac{8}{20} \left(\frac{c\ for\ conversion}{unknown\ c} = \frac{fl\ oz\ for\ conversion}{fl\ oz\ given}\right); \frac{x}{1} = \frac{20}{8} \left(\frac{unknown\ c}{c\ for\ conversion} = \frac{fl\ oz\ given}{fl\ oz\ for\ conversion}\right)$$

To solve a proportion, the ratios are cross-multiplied and the resulting equation is solved. When cross-multiplying, all four proportions above will produce the same equation: $(8)(x) = (20)(1) \rightarrow 8x = 20$. Dividing by 8 to isolate the variable *x*, the result is *x* = 2.5. The variable *x* represented the unknown number of cups. Therefore, the conclusion is that 20 fluid ounces converts (is equal) to 2.5 cups.

Sometimes converting units requires writing and solving more than one proportion. Suppose an exam question asks to determine how many hours are in 2 weeks. Without knowing the conversion rate between hours and weeks, this can be determined knowing the conversion rates between weeks and days, and between days and hours. First, weeks are converted to days, then days are converted to hours. To convert from weeks to days, the following proportion can be written:

$$\frac{7}{1} = \frac{x}{2} \left(\frac{days\ conversion}{weeks\ conversion} = \frac{days\ unknown}{weeks\ given}\right)$$

Cross-multiplying produces: $(7)(2) = (x)(1) \rightarrow 14 = x$. Therefore, 2 weeks is equal to 14 days. Next, a proportion is written to convert 14 days to hours: $\frac{24}{1} = \frac{x}{14} \left(\frac{conversion\ hours}{conversion\ days} = \frac{unknown\ hours}{given\ days}\right)$. Cross-multiplying produces: $(24)(14) = (x)(1) \rightarrow 336 = x$. Therefore, the answer is that there are 336 hours in 2 weeks.

Data Analysis/Probability

Measures of Center and Range

The center of a set of data (statistical values) can be represented by its mean, median, or mode. These are sometimes referred to as measures of central tendency. The mean is the average of the data set. The mean can be calculated by adding the data values and dividing by the sample size (the number of data points). Suppose a student has test scores of 93, 84, 88, 72, 91, and 77. To find the mean, or average, the scores are added and the sum is divided by 6 because there are 6 test scores:

$$\frac{93 + 84 + 88 + 72 + 91 + 77}{6} = \frac{505}{6} = 84.17$$

Given the mean of a data set and the sum of the data points, the sample size can be determined by dividing the sum by the mean. Suppose you are told that Kate averaged 12 points per game and scored a total of 156 points for the season. The number of games that she played (the sample size or the number of data points) can be determined by dividing the total points (sum of data points) by her average (mean of data points): $\frac{156}{12} = 13$. Therefore, Kate played in 13 games this season.

If given the mean of a data set and the sample size, the sum of the data points can be determined by multiplying the mean and sample size. Suppose you are told that Tom worked 6 days last week for an average of 5.5 hours per day. The total number of hours worked for the week (sum of data points) can be determined by multiplying his daily average (mean of data points) by the number of days worked (sample size): $5.5 \times 6 = 33$. Therefore, Tom worked a total of 33 hours last week.

The median of a data set is the value of the data point in the middle when the sample is arranged in numerical order. To find the median of a data set, the values are written in order from least to greatest. The lowest and highest values are simultaneously eliminated, repeating until the value in the middle remains. Suppose the salaries of math teachers are: $35,000; $38,500; $41,000; $42,000; $42,000; $44,500; $49,000. The values are listed from least to greatest to find the median. The lowest and highest values are eliminated until only the middle value remains. Repeating this step three times reveals a median salary of $42,000. If the sample set has an even number of data points, two values will remain after all others are eliminated. In this case, the mean of the two middle values is the median. Consider the following data set: 7, 9, 10, 13, 14, 14. Eliminating the lowest and highest values twice leaves two values, 10 and 13, in the middle. The mean of these values $\left(\frac{10+13}{2}\right)$ is the median. Therefore, the set has a median of 11.5.

The mode of a data set is the value that appears most often. A data set may have a single mode, multiple modes, or no mode. If different values repeat equally as often, multiple modes exist. If no value repeats, no mode exists. Consider the following data sets:

- A: 7, 9, 10, 13, 14, 14
- B: 37, 44, 33, 37, 49, 44, 51, 34, 37, 33, 44
- C: 173, 154, 151, 168, 155

Set A has a mode of 14. Set B has modes of 37 and 44. Set C has no mode.

The range of a data set is the difference between the highest and the lowest values in the set. The range can be considered the span of the data set. To determine the range, the smallest value in the set is subtracted from the largest value. The ranges for the data sets A, B, and C above are calculated as follows: A: $14 - 7 = 7$; B: $51 - 33 = 18$; C: $173 - 151 = 22$.

Best Description of a Set of Data
Measures of central tendency, namely mean, median, and mode, describe characteristics of a set of data. Specifically, they are intended to represent a *typical* value in the set by identifying a central position of the set. Depending on the characteristics of a specific set of data, different measures of central tendency are more indicative of a typical value in the set.

When a data set is grouped closely together with a relatively small range and the data is spread out somewhat evenly, the mean is an effective indicator of a typical value in the set. Consider the following data set representing the height of sixth grade boys in inches: 61 inches, 54 inches, 58 inches, 63 inches, 58 inches. The mean of the set is 58.8 inches. The data set is grouped closely (the range is only 9 inches) and the values are spread relatively evenly (three values below the mean and two values above the mean). Therefore, the mean value of 58.8 inches is an effective measure of central tendency in this case.

When a data set contains a small number of values either extremely large or extremely small when compared to the other values, the mean is not an effective measure of central tendency. Consider the following data set representing annual incomes of homeowners on a given street: $71,000; $74,000; $75,000; $77,000; $340,000. The mean of this set is $127,400. This figure does not indicate a typical value in the set, which contains four out of five values between $71,000 and $77,000. The median is a much more effective measure of central tendency for data sets such as these. Finding the middle value diminishes the influence of outliers, or numbers that may appear out of place, like the $340,000 annual income. The median for this set is $75,000 which is much more typical of a value in the set.

The mode of a data set is a useful measure of central tendency for categorical data when each piece of data is an option from a category. Consider a survey of 31 commuters asking how they get to work with results summarized below.

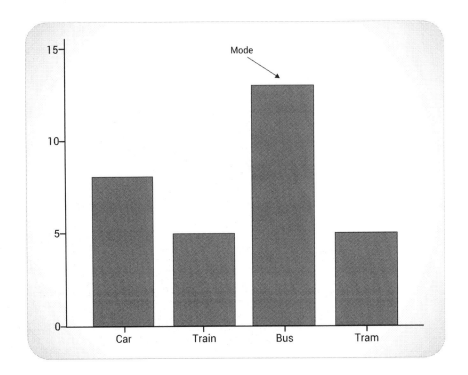

The mode for this set represents the value, or option, of the data that repeats most often. This indicates that the bus is the most popular method of transportation for the commuters.

Effects of Changes in Data
Changing all values of a data set in a consistent way produces predictable changes in the measures of the center and range of the set. A linear transformation changes the original value into the new value by either adding a given number to each value, multiplying each value by a given number, or both. Adding (or subtracting) a given value to each data point will increase (or decrease) the mean, median, and any modes by the same value. However, the range will remain the same due to the way that range is calculated. Multiplying (or dividing) a given value by each data point will increase (or decrease) the mean, median, and any modes, and the range by the same factor.

Consider the following data set, call it set P, representing the price of different cases of soda at a grocery store: $4.25, $4.40, $4.75, $4.95, $4.95, $5.15. The mean of set P is $4.74. The median is $4.85. The mode of the set is $4.95. The range is $0.90. Suppose the state passes a new tax of $0.25 on every case of soda sold. The new data set, set T, is calculated by adding $0.25 to each data point from set P. Therefore, set T consists of the following values: $4.50, $4.65, $5.00, $5.20, $5.20, $5.40. The mean of set T is $4.99. The median is $5.10. The mode of the set is $5.20. The range is $.90. The mean, median and mode of set T is equal to $0.25 added to the mean, median, and mode of set P. The range stays the same.

Now suppose, due to inflation, the store raises the cost of every item by 10 percent. Raising costs by 10 percent is calculated by multiplying each value by 1.1. The new data set, set *I*, is calculated by multiplying each data point from set *T* by 1.1. Therefore, set *I* consists of the following values: $4.95, $5.12, $5.50, $5.72, $5.72, $5.94. The mean of set *I* is $5.49. The median is $5.61. The mode of the set is $5.72. The range is $0.99. The mean, median, mode, and range of set *I* is equal to 1.1 multiplied by the mean, median, mode, and range of set *T* because each increased by a factor of 10 percent.

Describing a Set of Data

A set of data can be described in terms of its center, spread, shape and any unusual features. The center of a data set can be measured by its mean, median, or mode. Measures of central tendency are covered in the *Measures of Center and Range* section. The spread of a data set refers to how far the data points are from the center (mean or median). The spread can be measured by the range or the quartiles and interquartile range. A data set with data points clustered around the center will have a small spread. A data set covering a wide range will have a large spread.

When a data set is displayed as a histogram or frequency distribution plot, the shape indicates if a sample is normally distributed, symmetrical, or has measures of skewness or kurtosis. When graphed, a data set with a normal distribution will resemble a bell curve.

If the data set is symmetrical, each half of the graph when divided at the center is a mirror image of the other. If the graph has fewer data points to the right, the data is skewed right. If it has fewer data points to the left, the data is skewed left.

Right-Skewed   Symmetric   Left-Skewed

Kurtosis is a measure of whether the data is heavy-tailed with a high number of outliers, or light-tailed with a low number of outliers.

A description of a data set should include any unusual features such as gaps or outliers. A gap is a span within the range of the data set containing no data points. An outlier is a data point with a value either extremely large or extremely small when compared to the other values in the set.

Interpreting Displays of Data

A set of data can be visually displayed in various forms allowing for quick identification of characteristics of the set. Histograms, such as the one shown below, display the number of data points (vertical axis) that fall into given intervals (horizontal axis) across the range of the set. Suppose the histogram below displays IQ scores of students. Histograms can describe the center, spread, shape, and any unusual characteristics of a data set.

Histogram

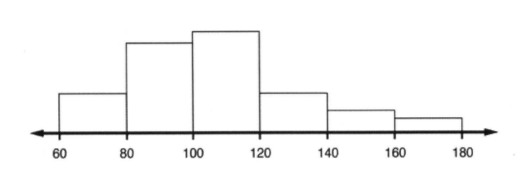

A box plot, also called a box-and-whisker plot, divides the data points into four groups and displays the five-number summary for the set, as well as any outliers. The five-number summary consists of:

- The lower extreme: the lowest value that is not an outlier
- The higher extreme: the highest value that is not an outlier
- The median of the set: also referred to as the second quartile or Q_2
- The first quartile or Q_1: the median of values below Q_2
- The third quartile or Q_3: the median of values above Q_2

Calculating each of these values is covered in the next section, *Graphical Representation of Data*.

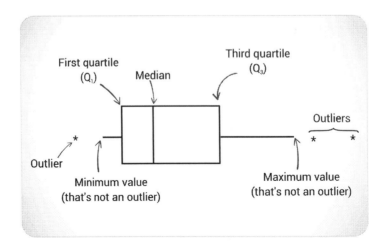

Suppose the box plot displays IQ scores for 12th grade students at a given school. The five number summary of the data consists of: lower extreme (67); upper extreme (127); Q_2 or median (100); Q_1 (91); Q_3 (108); and outliers (135 and 140). Although all data points are not known from the plot, the points are divided into four quartiles each, including 25% of the data points. Therefore, 25% of students scored between 67 and 91, 25% scored between 91 and 100, 25% scored between 100 and 108, and 25% scored between 108 and 127. These percentages include the normal values for the set and exclude the outliers. This information is useful when comparing a given score with the rest of the scores in the set.

A scatter plot is a mathematical diagram that visually displays the relationship or connection between two variables. The independent variable is placed on the x-axis, or horizontal axis, and the dependent variable is placed on the y-axis, or vertical axis. When visually examining the points on the graph, if the points model a linear relationship, or a line of best-fit can be drawn through the points with the points relatively close on either side, then a correlation exists. If the line of best-fit has a positive slope (rises from left to right), then the variables have a positive correlation. If the line of best-fit has a negative slope (falls from left to right), then the variables have a negative correlation. If a line of best-fit cannot be drawn, then no correlation exists. A positive or negative correlation can be categorized as strong or weak, depending on how closely the points are graphed around the line of best-fit.

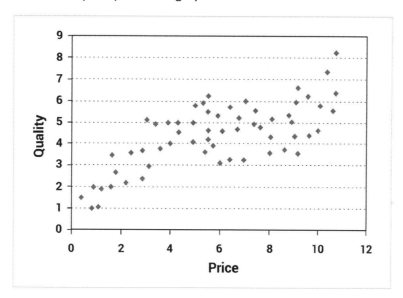

Graphical Representation of Data

Various graphs can be used to visually represent a given set of data. Each type of graph requires a different method of arranging data points and different calculations of the data. Examples of histograms, box plots, and scatter plots are discussed in the previous section *Interpreting Displays of Data*. To construct a histogram, the range of the data points is divided into equal intervals. The frequency for each interval is then determined, which reveals how many points fall into each interval. A graph is constructed with the vertical axis representing the frequency and the horizontal axis representing the intervals. The lower value of each interval should be labeled along the horizontal axis. Finally, for each interval, a bar is drawn from the lower value of each interval to the lower value of the next interval with a height equal to the frequency of the interval. Because of the intervals, histograms do not have any gaps between bars along the horizontal axis.

A scatter plot displays the relationship between two variables. Values for the independent variable, typically denoted by x, are paired with values for the dependent variable, typically denoted by y. Each set of corresponding values are written as an ordered pair (*x*, *y*). To construct the graph, a coordinate grid is labeled with the *x*-axis representing the independent variable and the *y*-axis representing the dependent variable. Each ordered pair is graphed.

Like a scatter plot, a line graph compares variables that change continuously, typically over time. Paired data values (ordered pair) are plotted on a coordinate grid with the *x*- and *y*-axis representing the variables. A line is drawn from each point to the next, going from left to right. The line graph below displays cell phone use for given years (two variables) for men, women, and both sexes (three data sets).

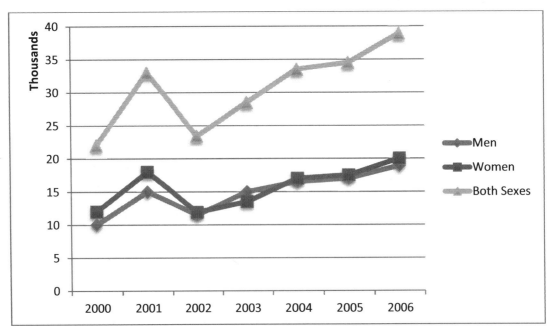

50

A line plot, also called dot plot, displays the frequency of data (numerical values) on a number line. To construct a line plot, a number line is used that includes all unique data values. It is marked with x's or dots above the value the number of times that the value occurs in the data set.

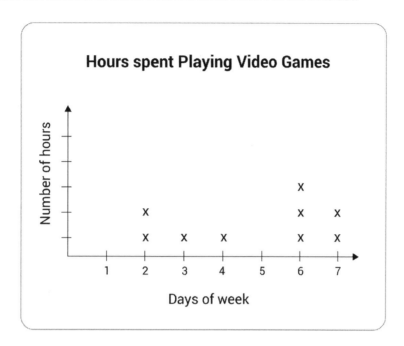

A bar graph looks similar to a histogram but displays categorical data. The horizontal axis represents each category and the vertical axis represents the frequency for the category. A bar is drawn for each category (often different colors) with a height extending to the frequency for that category within the data set. A double bar graph displays two sets of data that contain data points consisting of the same categories. The double bar graph below indicates that two girls and four boys like Pad Thai the most out of all the foods, two boys and five girls like pizza, and so on.

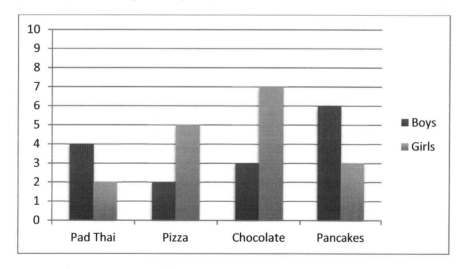

A circle graph, also called a pie chart, displays categorical data with each category representing a percentage of the whole data set. To construct a circle graph, the percent of the data set for each category must be determined. To do so, the frequency of the category is divided by the total number of data points and converted to a percent. For example, if 80 people were asked their favorite pizza topping and 20 responded cheese, then cheese constitutes 25% of the data ($\frac{20}{80} = .25 = 25\%$). Each category in a data set is represented by a *slice* of the circle proportionate to its percentage of the whole.

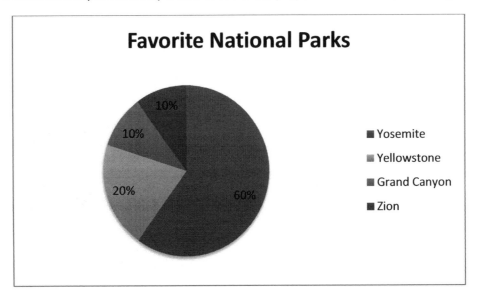

Choice of Graphs to Display Data

Choosing the appropriate graph to display a data set depends on what type of data is included in the set and what information must be displayed. Histograms and box plots can be used for data sets consisting of individual values across a wide range. Examples include test scores and incomes. Histograms and box plots will indicate the center, spread, range, and outliers of a data set. A histogram will show the shape of the data set, while a box plot will divide the set into quartiles (25% increments), allowing for comparison between a given value and the entire set.

Scatter plots and line graphs can be used to display data consisting of two variables. Examples include height and weight, or distance and time. A correlation between the variables is determined by examining the points on the graph. Line graphs are used if each value for one variable pairs with a distinct value for the other variable. Line graphs show relationships between variables.

Line plots, bar graphs, and circle graphs are all used to display categorical data, such as surveys. Line plots and bar graphs both indicate the frequency of each category within the data set. A line plot is used when the categories consist of numerical values. For example, the number of hours of TV watched by individuals is displayed on a line plot. A bar graph is used when the categories consists of words. For example, the favorite ice cream of individuals is displayed with a bar graph. A circle graph can be used to display either type of categorical data. However, unlike line plots and bar graphs, a circle graph does not indicate the frequency of each category. Instead, the circle graph represents each category as its percentage of the whole data set.

Probabilities Relative to Likelihood of Occurrence

Probability is a measure of how likely an event is to occur. Probability is written as a fraction between zero and one. If an event has a probability of zero, the event will never occur. If an event has a probability of one, the event will definitely occur. If the probability of an event is closer to zero, the event is unlikely to occur. If the probability of an event is closer to one, the event is more likely to occur. For example, a probability of $\frac{1}{2}$ means that the event is equally as likely to occur as it is not to occur. An example of this is tossing a coin. To calculate the probability of an event, the number of favorable outcomes is divided by the number of total outcomes. For example, suppose you have 2 raffle tickets out of 20 total tickets sold. The probability that you win the raffle is calculated: $\frac{number\ of\ favorable\ outcomes}{total\ number of\ outcomes} = \frac{2}{20} = \frac{1}{10}$ (always reduce fractions). Therefore, the probability of winning the raffle is $\frac{1}{10}$ or 0.1.

Chance is the measure of how likely an event is to occur, written as a percent. If an event will never occur, the event has a 0% chance. If an event will certainly occur, the event has a 100% chance. If an event will sometimes occur, the event has a chance somewhere between 0% and 100%. To calculate chance, probability is calculated and the fraction is converted to a percent.

The probability of multiple events occurring can be determined by multiplying the probability of each event. For example, suppose you flip a coin with heads and tails, and roll a six-sided dice numbered one through six. To find the probability that you will flip heads AND roll a two, the probability of each event is determined and those fractions are multiplied. The probability of flipping heads is $\frac{1}{2} \left(\frac{1\ side\ with\ heads}{2\ sides\ total} \right)$ and the probability of rolling a two is $\frac{1}{6} \left(\frac{1\ side\ with\ a\ 2}{6\ total\ sides} \right)$. The probability of flipping heads AND rolling a 2 is: $\frac{1}{2} \times \frac{1}{6} = \frac{1}{12}$.

The above scenario with flipping a coin and rolling a dice is an example of independent events. Independent events are circumstances in which the outcome of one event does not affect the outcome of the other event. Conversely, dependent events are ones in which the outcome of one event affects the outcome of the second event. Consider the following scenario: a bag contains 5 black marbles and 5 white marbles. What is the probability of picking 2 black marbles without replacing the marble after the first pick?

The probability of picking a black marble on the first pick is $\frac{5}{10} \left(\frac{5\ black\ marbles}{10\ total\ marbles} \right)$. Assuming that a black marble was picked, there are now 4 black marbles and 5 white marbles for the second pick. Therefore, the probability of picking a black marble on the second pick is $\frac{4}{9} \left(\frac{4\ black\ marbles}{9\ total\ marbles} \right)$. To find the probability of picking two black marbles, the probability of each is multiplied: $\frac{5}{10} \times \frac{4}{9} = \frac{20}{90} = \frac{2}{9}$.

Practice Questions

1. Which of the following is equivalent to the value of the digit 3 in the number 792.134?
   a. 3×10
   b. 3×100
   c. $\frac{3}{10}$
   d. $\frac{3}{100}$ *(circled)*

2. How will the following number be written in standard form: $(1 \times 10^4) + (3 \times 10^3) + (7 \times 10^1) + (8 \times 10^0)$
   a. 137
   b. 13,078 *(circled)*
   c. 1,378
   d. 8,731

   100×100 13072

   $10000 + 3000$

3. How will the number 847.89632 be written if rounded to the nearest hundredth?
   a. 847.90 *(circled)*
   b. 900
   c. 847.89
   d. 847.896

   847.90

4. What is the value of the sum of $\frac{1}{3}$ and $\frac{2}{5}$?
   a. $\frac{3}{8}$
   b. $\frac{11}{15}$ *(circled)*
   c. $\frac{11}{30}$
   d. $\frac{4}{5}$

   $\frac{1}{3} + \frac{2}{5}$

5. What is the value of the expression: $7^2 - 3 \times (4 + 2) + 15 \div 5$?
   a. 12.2
   b. 40.2
   c. 34 *(circled)*
   d. 58.2

   $49 - 18 + 3$
   $49 - 15$

6. How will $\frac{4}{5}$ be written as a percent?
   a. 40%
   b. 125%
   c. 90%
   d. 80% *(circled)*

   $\frac{80}{100}$

7. If Danny takes 48 minutes to walk 3 miles, how long should it take him to walk 5 miles maintaining the same speed?
   - a. 32 min
   - b. 64 min
   - (c.) 80 min
   - d. 96 min

$$\frac{16}{3\overline{)48}}$$
$$\frac{3}{18}$$

$$\frac{16}{\times 5}$$
$$\overline{80}$$

8. What are all the factors of 12?
   - a. 12, 24, 36
   - b. 1, 2, 4, 6, 12
   - c. 12, 24, 36, 48
   - (d.) 1, 2, 3, 4, 6, 12

9. A construction company is building a new housing development with the property of each house measuring 30 feet wide. If the length of the street is zoned off at 345 feet, how many houses can be built on the street?
   - (a.) 11
   - b. 115
   - c. 11.5
   - d. 12

$$11\ 1 RS$$
$$30\overline{)345}$$
$$\frac{30}{45}$$
$$\frac{30}{}$$

10. How will the following algebraic expression be simplified: $(5x^2 - 3x + 4) - (2x^2 - 7)$?
   - a. x^5
   - (b.) $3x^2 - 3x + 11$
   - c. $3x^2 - 3x - 3$
   - d. $x - 3$

$$5x^2 - 3x + 4 - 2x^2 + 7 = 3x^2 - 3x + 11$$

11. Kassidy drove for 3 hours at a speed of 60 miles per hour. Using the distance formula, $d = r \times t$ (*distance* $= rate \times time$), how far did Kassidy travel?
   - a. 20 miles
   - (b.) 180 miles
   - c. 65 miles
   - d. 120 miles

$$x = 60 \times 3$$

$$-3x - 12 \geq x + 8$$
$$-20 \geq 4x$$
$$\overline{\ }$$
$$-5 \geq x$$

12. If $-3(x + 4) \geq x + 8$, what is the value of x?
   - a. $x = 4$
   - b. $x \geq 2$
   - (c.) $x \geq -5$
   - (d.) $x \leq -5$

$$-3x - 12 \geq x + 8$$
$$-x \qquad -x$$

$$-4x - 12 \geq 8$$

$$-3x - 12 \geq x + 8$$
$$-x + 12 \quad -x + 12$$
$$-4x \leq 20$$
$$\boxed{x \leq -5}$$

$$-3 + 12 > 9$$
$$-15 \geq 9$$

$$-3x - 12 \quad x + 8$$
$$+12 \qquad +12$$
$$-x \qquad -3x$$
$$-4x \geq 20$$
$$x = -5$$

why does this need to switch

when rely then I divide by - I have to flip sign #

55

13. Karen gets paid a weekly salary and a commission for every sale that she makes. The table below shows the number of sales and her pay for different weeks.

Sales	2	7	4	8
Pay	$380	$580	$460	$620

Which of the following equations represents Karen's weekly pay?

a. $y = 90x + 200$ ✓
b. $y = 90x - 200$
c. $y = 40x + 300$ ✓
d. $y = 40x - 300$

commission paid for selling

14. Which inequality represents the values displayed on the number line?

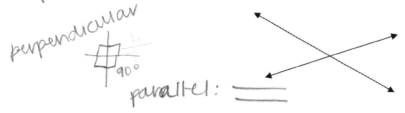

a. $x < 1$
b. $x \leq 1$
c. $x > 1$
d. $x \geq 1$

○ = < ?

● ≤ ?

15. What is the 42nd item in the pattern: ▲○○□ ▲○○□ ▲ ...?

a. ○
b. ▲
c. □
d. None of the above

$4 \overline{)42}$ → 10

16. Which of the following statements is true about the two lines below?

perpendicular

90°

parallel: ═══

a. The two lines are parallel but not perpendicular.
b. The two lines are perpendicular but not parallel.
c. The two lines are both parallel and perpendicular.
d. The two lines are neither parallel nor perpendicular.

17. Which of the following figures is not a polygon?

a. Decagon
b. Cone
c. Triangle
d. Rhombus

18. What is the area of the regular hexagon shown below?

10.39

12

a. 72
b. 124.68
c. 374.04
d. 748.08

$A = \frac{1}{2} \cdot b \cdot h$

$= \frac{1}{2} \cdot 12 \cdot 10.39$

$6 \times 60 = 360$

$= 6 \times 10.39$

$= \boxed{60}$

19. The area of a given rectangle is 24 centimeters. If the measure of each side is multiplied by 3, what is the area of the new figure?
a. 48cm
b. 72cm
c. 216cm
d. 13,824cm

$24 \times 3^2 = 216$

$\overline{24}$

$\frac{24}{3}$

$\overline{72}$

$\frac{24}{4}$

$\frac{}{9}$

3X

3X ☐

9X

$X \cdot X = 24$

20. What are the coordinates of the point plotted on the grid?

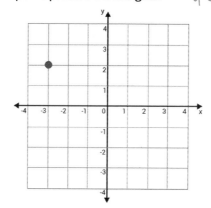

a. (-3, 2)
b. (2, -3)
c. (-3, -2)
d. (2, 3)

21. The perimeter of a 6-sided polygon is 56 cm. The length of three sides is 9 cm each. The length of two other sides is 8 cm each. What is the length of the missing side?
a. 11 cm
b. 12 cm
c. 13 cm
d. 10 cm

$9 + 9 + 9 + 8 + 8 = 43$

$\frac{27}{16}$

$\overline{43}$

$P = 56$

$\begin{array}{r} 56 \\ -43 \\ \hline 13 \end{array}$

$56 - 43 = 13$

57

22. Katie works at a clothing company and sold 192 shirts over the weekend. $1/3$ of the shirts that were sold were patterned, and the rest were solid. Which mathematical expression would calculate the number of solid shirts Katie sold over the weekend?

a. $192 \times \frac{1}{3}$

b. $192 \div \frac{1}{3}$

c. $192 \times (1 - \frac{1}{3})$

d. $192 \div 3$

23. Which measure for the center of a small sample set is most affected by outliers?
   a. Mean
   b. Median
   c. Mode
   d. None of the above

24. Given the value of a given stock at monthly intervals, which graph should be used to best represent the trend of the stock?
   a. Box plot
   b. Line plot
   c. Line graph
   d. Circle graph

25. What is the probability of randomly picking the winner and runner-up from a race of 4 horses and distinguishing which is the winner?
   a. $\frac{1}{4}$

   b. $\frac{1}{2}$

   c. $\frac{1}{16}$

   d. $\frac{1}{12}$

26. Which of the following numbers has the greatest value?
   a. 1.4378
   b. 1.07548
   c. 1.43592
   d. 0.89409

27. The value of 6 x 12 is the same as:
   a. 2 x 4 x 4 x 2
   b. 7 x 4 x 3
   c. 6 x 6 x 3
   d. 3 x 3 x 4 x 2

28. This chart indicates how many sales of CDs, vinyl records, and MP3 downloads occurred over the last year. Approximately what percentage of the total sales was from CDs?

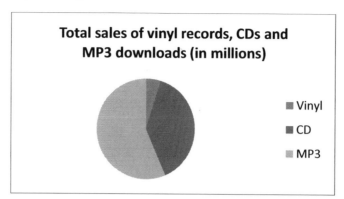

a. 55%
b. 25%
c. 40%
d. 5%

29. After a 20% sale discount, Frank purchased a new refrigerator for $850. How much did he save from the original price?
a. $170
b. $212.50
c. $105.75
d. $200

30. Which of the following is largest?
a. 0.45
b. 0.096
c. 0.3
d. 0.313

31. What is the value of *b* in this equation?

$$5b - 4 = 2b + 17$$

a. 13
b. 24
c. 7
d. 21

32. A school has 15 teachers and 20 teaching assistants. They have 200 students. What is the ratio of faculty to students?
a. 3:20
b. 4:17
c. 3:2
d. 7:40

33. Express the solution to the following problem in decimal form:

$$\frac{3}{5} \times \frac{7}{10} \div \frac{1}{2}$$

    a. 0.042
    b. 84%
    c. 0.84
    d. 0.42

34. A student gets an 85% on a test with 20 questions. How many answers did the student solve correctly?
    a. 15
    b. 16
    c. 17
    d. 18

35. If Sarah reads at an average rate of 21 pages in four nights, how long will it take her to read 140 pages?
    a. 6 nights
    b. 26 nights
    c. 8 nights
    d. 27 nights

36. Alan currently weighs 200 pounds, but he wants to lose weight to get down to 175 pounds. What is this difference in kilograms? (1 pound is approximately equal to 0.45 kilograms.)
    a. 9 kg
    b. 11.25 kg
    c. 78.75 kg
    d. 90 kg

37. Johnny earns $2334.50 from his job each month. He pays $1437 for monthly expenses. Johnny is planning a vacation in 3 months' time that he estimates will cost $1750 total. How much will Johnny have left over from three months' of saving once he pays for his vacation?
    a. $948.50
    b. $584.50
    c. $852.50
    d. $942.50

38. What is $\frac{420}{98}$ rounded to the nearest integer?
    a. 3
    b. 4
    c. 5
    d. 6

39. Solve the following:

$$4 \times 7 + (25 - 21)^2 \div 2$$

    a. 512
    b. 36
    c. 60.5
    d. 22

40. The total perimeter of a rectangle is 36 cm. If the length of each side is 12 cm, what is the width?
    a. 3 cm
    b. 12 cm
    c. 6 cm
    d. 8 cm

41. Dwayne has received the following scores on his math tests: 78, 92, 83, 97. What score must Dwayne get on his next math test to have an overall average of at least 90?
    a. 89
    b. 98
    c. 95
    d. 100

42. What is the overall median of Dwayne's current scores: 78, 92, 83, 97?
    a. 19
    b. 85
    c. 83
    d. 87.5

43. Solve the following:

$$\left(\sqrt{36} \times \sqrt{16}\right) - 3^2$$

    a. 30
    b. 21
    c. 15
    d. 13

44. In Jim's school, there are 3 girls for every 2 boys. There are 650 students in total. Using this information, how many students are girls?
    a. 260
    b. 130
    c. 65
    d. 390

45. What is the solution to $4 \times 7 + (25 - 21)^2 \div 2$?
    a. 512
    b. 36
    c. 60.5
    d. 22

46. Kimberley earns $10 an hour babysitting, and after 10 p.m., she earns $12 an hour, with the amount paid being rounded to the nearest hour accordingly. On her last job, she worked from 5:30 p.m. to 11 p.m. In total, how much did Kimberley earn on her last job?

   a. $45
   b. $57
   c. $62
   d. $42

47. Solve this equation:

$$9x + x - 7 = 16 + 2x$$

   a. -4

   b. 3

   c. $\frac{9}{8}$

   d. $\frac{23}{8}$

48. Arrange the following numbers from least to greatest value:
   $0.85, \frac{4}{5}, \frac{2}{3}, \frac{91}{100}$

   a. $0.85, \frac{4}{5}, \frac{2}{3}, \frac{91}{100}$

   b. $\frac{4}{5}, 0.85, \frac{91}{100}, \frac{2}{3}$

   c. $\frac{2}{3}, \frac{4}{5}, 0.85, \frac{91}{100}$

   d. $0.85, \frac{91}{100}, \frac{4}{5}, \frac{2}{3}$

49. Keith's bakery had 252 customers go through its doors last week. This week, that number increased to 378. Express this increase as a percentage.
   a. 26%
   b. 50%
   c. 35%
   d. 12%

50. If $4x - 3 = 5$, then $x =$
   a. 1
   b. 2
   c. 3
   d. 4

Answer Explanations

1. D: $\frac{3}{100}$. Each digit to the left of the decimal point represents a higher multiple of 10 and each digit to the right of the decimal point represents a quotient of a higher multiple of 10 for the divisor. The first digit to the right of the decimal point is equal to the value ÷ 10. The second digit to the right of the decimal point is equal to the value ÷ (10 × 10), or the value ÷ 100.

2. B: 13,078. The power of 10 by which a digit is multiplied corresponds with the number of zeros following the digit when expressing its value in standard form. Therefore, $(1 \times 10^4) + (3 \times 10^3) + (7 \times 10^1) + (8 \times 10^0) = 10{,}000 + 3{,}000 + 70 + 8 = 13{,}078$.

3. A: 847.90. The hundredths place value is located two digits to the right of the decimal point (the digit 9). The digit to the right of the place value is examined to decide whether to round up or keep the digit. In this case, the digit 6 is 5 or greater so the hundredth place is rounded up. When rounding up, if the digit to be increased is a 9, the digit to its left is increased by one and the digit in the desired place value is made a zero. Therefore, the number is rounded to 847.90.

4. B: $\frac{11}{15}$. Fractions must have like denominators to be added. The least common multiple of the denominators 3 and 5 is found. The LCM is 15, so both fractions should be changed to equivalent fractions with a denominator of 15. To determine the numerator of the new fraction, the old numerator is multiplied by the same number by which the old denominator is multiplied to obtain the new denominator. For the fraction $\frac{1}{3}$, 3 multiplied by 5 will produce 15. Therefore, the numerator is multiplied by 5 to produce the new numerator $\left(\frac{1 \times 5}{3 \times 5} = \frac{5}{15}\right)$. For the fraction $\frac{2}{5}$, multiplying both the numerator and denominator by 3 produces $\frac{6}{15}$. When fractions have like denominators, they are added by adding the numerators and keeping the denominator the same: $\frac{5}{15} + \frac{6}{15} = \frac{11}{15}$.

5. C: 34. When performing calculations consisting of more than one operation, the order of operations should be followed: *Parenthesis, Exponents, Multiplication/Division, Addition/Subtraction*. Parenthesis: $7^2 - 3 \times (4 + 2) + 15 \div 5 = 7^2 - 3 \times (6) + 15 \div 5$. Exponents: $7^2 - 3 \times 6 + 15 \div 5 = 49 - 3 \times 6 + 15 \div 5$. Multiplication/Division (from left to right): $49 - 3 \times 6 + 15 \div 5 = 49 - 18 + 3$. Addition/Subtraction (from left to right): $49 - 18 + 3 = 34$.

6. D: 80%. To convert a fraction to a percent, the fraction is first converted to a decimal. To do so, the numerator is divided by the denominator: $4 \div 5 = 0.8$. To convert a decimal to a percent, the number is multiplied by 100: $0.8 \times 100 = 80\%$.

7. C: 80 min. To solve the problem, a proportion is written consisting of ratios comparing distance and time. One way to set up the proportion is: $\frac{3}{48} = \frac{5}{x} \left(\frac{distance}{time} = \frac{distance}{time}\right)$ where x represents the unknown value of time. To solve a proportion, the ratios are cross-multiplied: $(3)(x) = (5)(48) \rightarrow 3x = 240$. The equation is solved by isolating the variable, or dividing by 3 on both sides, to produce $x = 80$.

8. D: 1, 2, 3, 4, 6, 12. A given number divides evenly by each of its factors to produce an integer (no decimals). The number 5, 7, 8, 9, 10, 11 (and their opposites) do not divide evenly into 12. Therefore, these numbers are not factors.

9. A: 11. To determine the number of houses that can fit on the street, the length of the street is divided by the width of each house: $345 \div 30 = 11.5$. Although the mathematical calculation of 11.5 is correct, this answer is not reasonable. Half of a house cannot be built, so the company will need to either build 11 or 12 houses. Since the width of 12 houses (360 feet) will extend past the length of the street, only 11 houses can be built.

10. B: $3x^2 - 3x + 11$. By distributing the implied one in front of the first set of parentheses and the -1 in front of the second set of parentheses, the parenthesis can be eliminated: $1(5x^2 - 3x + 4) - 1(2x^2 - 7) = 5x^2 - 3x + 4 - 2x^2 + 7$. Next, like terms (same variables with same exponents) are combined by adding the coefficients and keeping the variables and their powers the same: $5x^2 - 3x + 4 - 2x^2 + 7 = 3x^2 - 3x + 11$.

11. B: 180 miles. The rate, 60 miles per hour, and time, 3 hours, are given for the scenario. To determine the distance traveled, the given values for the rate (r) and time (t) are substituted into the distance formula and evaluated: $d = r \times t \rightarrow d = (60mi/h) \times (3h) \rightarrow d = 180mi$.

12. D: $x \leq -5$. When solving a linear equation or inequality:

Distribution is performed if necessary: $-3(x + 4) \rightarrow -3x - 12 \geq x + 8$. This means that any like terms on the same side of the equation/inequality are combined.

The equation/inequality is manipulated to get the variable on one side. In this case, subtracting x from both sides produces $-4x - 12 \geq 8$.

The variable is isolated using inverse operations to undo addition/subtraction. Adding 12 to both sides produces $-4x \geq 20$.

The variable is isolated using inverse operations to undo multiplication/division. Remember if dividing by a negative number, the relationship of the inequality reverses, so the sign is flipped. In this case, dividing by -4 on both sides produces $x \leq -5$.

13. C: $y = 40x + 300$. In this scenario, the variables are the number of sales and Karen's weekly pay. The weekly pay depends on the number of sales. Therefore, weekly pay is the dependent variable (y) and the number of sales is the independent variable (x). Each pair of values from the table can be written as an ordered pair (x, y): (2,380), (7,580), (4,460), (8,620). The ordered pairs can be substituted into the equations to see which creates true statements (both sides equal) for each pair. Even if one ordered pair produces equal values for a given equation, the other three ordered pairs must be checked. The only equation which is true for all four ordered pairs is $y = 40x + 300$:

$$380 = 40(2) + 300 \rightarrow 380 = 380$$

$$580 = 40(7) + 300 \rightarrow 580 = 580$$

$$460 = 40(4) + 300 \rightarrow 460 = 460$$

$$620 = 40(8) + 300 \rightarrow 620 = 620$$

14. D: $x \geq 1$. The closed dot on one indicates that the value is included in the set. The arrow pointing right indicates that numbers greater than one (numbers get larger to the right) are included in the set. Therefore, the set includes numbers greater than or equal to one, which can be written as $x \geq 1$.

15. A: ○. The core of the pattern consists of 4 items: ▲○○□. Therefore, the core repeats in multiples of 4, with the pattern starting over on the next step. The closest multiple of 4 to 42 is 40. Step 40 is the end of the core (□), so step 41 will start the core over (▲) and step 42 is ○.

16. D: The two lines are neither parallel nor perpendicular. Parallel lines will never intersect or meet. Therefore, the lines are not parallel. Perpendicular lines intersect to form a right angle (90°). Although the lines intersect, they do not form a right angle, which is usually indicated with a box at the intersection point. Therefore, the lines are not perpendicular.

17. B: Cone. A polygon is a closed two-dimensional figure consisting of three or more sides. A decagon is a polygon with 10 sides. A triangle is a polygon with three sides. A rhombus is a polygon with 4 sides. A cone is a three-dimensional figure and is classified as a solid.

18. C: 374.04. The formula for finding the area of a regular polygon is $A = \frac{1}{2} \times a \times P$ where a is the length of the apothem (from the center to any side at a right angle) and P is the perimeter of the figure. The apothem a is given as 10.39 and the perimeter can be found by multiplying the length of one side by the number of sides (since the polygon is regular): $P = 12 \times 6 \rightarrow P = 72$. To find the area, substitute the values for a and P into the formula $A = \frac{1}{2} \times a \times P \rightarrow A = \frac{1}{2} \times (10.39) \times (72) \rightarrow A = 374.04$.

19. C: 216cm. Because area is a two-dimensional measurement, the dimensions are multiplied by a scale that is squared to determine the scale of the corresponding areas. The dimensions of the rectangle are multiplied by a scale of 3. Therefore, the area is multiplied by a scale of 3^2 (which is equal to 9): $24cm \times 9 = 216cm$.

20. A: (-3, 2). The coordinates of a point are written as an ordered pair (x, y). To determine the x-coordinate, a line is traced directly above or below the point until reaching the x-axis. This step notes the value on the x-axis. In this case, the x-coordinate is -3. To determine the y-coordinate, a line is traced directly to the right or left of the point until reaching the y-axis, which notes the value on the y-axis. In this case, the y-coordinate is 2. Therefore, the ordered pair is written (-3, 2).

21. C: Perimeter is found by calculating the sum of all sides of the polygon. $9 + 9 + 9 + 8 + 8 + s = 56$, where s is the missing side length. Therefore, 43 plus the missing side length is equal to 56. The missing side length is 13 cm.

22. C: $\frac{1}{3}$ of the shirts sold were patterned. Therefore, $1 - \frac{1}{3} = \frac{2}{3}$ of the shirts sold were solid. Anytime "of" a quantity appears in a word problem, multiplication should be used. Therefore, $192 \times \frac{2}{3} = \frac{192 \times 2}{3} = \frac{384}{3} = 128$ solid shirts were sold. The entire expression is $192 \times \left(1 - \frac{1}{3}\right)$.

23. A: Mean. An outlier is a data value that is either far above or far below the majority of values in a sample set. The mean is the average of all the values in the set. In a small sample set, a very high or very low number could drastically change the average of the data points. Outliers will have no more of an effect on the median (the middle value when arranged from lowest to highest) than any other value above or below the median. If the same outlier does not repeat, outliers will have no effect on the mode (value that repeats most often).

24. C: Line graph. The scenario involves data consisting of two variables, month, and stock value. Box plots display data consisting of values for one variable. Therefore, a box plot is not an appropriate choice. Both line plots and circle graphs are used to display frequencies within categorical data. Neither can be used for the given scenario. Line graphs display two numerical variables on a coordinate grid and show trends among the variables.

25. D: $\frac{1}{12}$. The probability of picking the winner of the race is $\frac{1}{4}$ $\left(\frac{number\ of\ favorable\ outcomes}{number\ of\ total\ outcomes}\right)$. Assuming the winner was picked on the first selection, three horses remain from which to choose the runner-up (these are dependent events). Therefore, the probability of picking the runner-up is $\frac{1}{3}$. To determine the probability of multiple events, the probability of each event is multiplied: $\frac{1}{4} \times \frac{1}{3} = \frac{1}{12}$.

26. A: Compare each numeral after the decimal point to figure out which overall number is greatest. In answers A (1.43785) and C (1.43592), both have the same tenths (4) and hundredths (3). However, the thousandths is greater in answer A (7), so A has the greatest value overall.

27. D: By grouping the four numbers in the answer into factors of the two numbers of the question (6 and 12), it can be determined that (3 x 2) x (4 x 3) = 6 x 12. Alternatively, each of the answer choices could be prime factored or multiplied out and compared to the original value. 6×12 has a value of 72 and a prime factorization of $2^3 \times 3^2$. The answer choices respectively have values of 64, 84, 108, and 72 and prime factorizations of 2^6, $2^2 \times 3 \times 7$, $2^2 \times 3^3$, and $2^3 \times 3^2$, so answer D is the correct choice.

28. C: The sum total percentage of a pie chart must equal 100%. Since the CD sales take up less than half of the chart and more than a quarter (25%), it can be determined to be 40% overall. This can also be measured with a protractor. The angle of a circle is 360°. Since 25% of 360 would be 90° and 50% would be 180°, the angle percentage of CD sales falls in between; therefore, it would be answer C.

29. B: Since $850 is the price *after* a 20% discount, $850 represents 80% of the original price. To determine the original price, set up a proportion with the ratio of the sale price (850) to original price (unknown) equal to the ratio of sale percentage:

$$\frac{850}{x} = \frac{80}{100}$$

(where x represents the unknown original price)

To solve a proportion, cross multiply the numerators and denominators and set the products equal to each other: (850)(100) = (80)(x). Multiplying each side results in the equation 85,000=80x.

To solve for x, divide both sides by 80: $\frac{85,000}{80} = \frac{80x}{80}$, resulting in x=1062.5. Remember that x represents the original price. Subtracting the sale price from the original price ($1062.50-$850) indicates that Frank saved $212.50.

30. A: To figure out which is largest, look at the first non-zero digits. Answer B's first nonzero digit is in the hundredths place. The other three all have nonzero digits in the tenths place, so it must be A, C, or D. Of these, A has the largest first nonzero digit.

31. C: To solve for the value of b, both sides of the equation need to be equalized.

Start by cancelling out the lower value of -4 by adding 4 to both sides:

$$5b - 4 = 2b + 17$$

$$5b - 4 + 4 = 2b + 17 + 4$$

$$5b = 2b + 21$$

The variable *b* is the same on each side, so subtract the lower 2b from each side:

$$5b = 2b + 21$$

$$5b - 2b = 2b + 21 - 2b$$

$$3b = 21$$

Then divide both sides by 3 to get the value of *b*:

$$3b = 21$$

$$\frac{3b}{3} = \frac{21}{3}$$

$$b = 7$$

32. D: The total faculty is 15 + 20 = 35. So the ratio is 35:200. Then, divide both of these numbers by 5, since 5 is a common factor to both, with a result of 7:40.

33. C: The first step in solving this problem is expressing the result in fraction form. Separate this problem first by solving the division operation of the last two fractions. When dividing one fraction by another, invert or flip the second fraction and then multiply the numerator and denominator.

$$\frac{7}{10} \times \frac{2}{1} = \frac{14}{10}$$

Next, multiply the first fraction with this value:

$$\frac{3}{5} \times \frac{14}{10} = \frac{42}{50}$$

Decimals are expressions of 1 or 100%, so multiply both the numerator and denominator by 2 to get the fraction as an expression of 100.

$$\frac{42}{50} \times \frac{2}{2} = \frac{84}{100}$$

In decimal form, this would be expressed as 0.84.

34. C: 85% of a number means that number should be multiplied by 0.85: $0.85 \times 20 = \frac{85}{100} \times \frac{20}{1}$, which can be simplified to $\frac{17}{20} \times \frac{20}{1} = 17$. The answer is *C*.

35. D: This problem can be solved by setting up a proportion involving the given information and the unknown value. The proportion is:

$$\frac{21 \; pages}{4 \; nights} = \frac{140 \; pages}{x \; nights}$$

Solving the proportion by cross-multiplying, the equation becomes $21x = 4 * 140$, where $x = 26.67$. Since it is not an exact number of nights, the answer is rounded up to 27 nights. Twenty-six nights would not give Sarah enough time.

36. B: Using the conversion rate, multiply the projected weight loss of 25 lb by $0.45 \frac{kg}{lb}$ to get the amount in kilograms (11.25 kg).

37. D: First, subtract $1437 from $2334.50 to find Johnny's monthly savings; this equals $897.50. Then, multiply this amount by 3 to find out how much he will have (in three months) before he pays for his vacation: this equals $2692.50. Finally, subtract the cost of the vacation ($1750) from this amount to find how much Johnny will have left: $942.50.

38. B: Dividing by 98 can be approximated by dividing by 100, which would mean shifting the decimal point of the numerator to the left by 2. The result is 4.2 which rounds to 4.

39. B: To solve this correctly, keep in mind the order of operations with the mnemonic PEMDAS (Please Excuse My Dear Aunt Sally). This stands for Parentheses, Exponents, Multiplication, Division, Addition, Subtraction. Taking it step by step, solve the parentheses first:

$$4 \times 7 + (4)^2 \div 2$$

Then, apply the exponent:

$$4 \times 7 + 16 \div 2$$

Multiplication and division are both performed next:

$$28 + 8 = 36$$

40. C: The formula for the perimeter of a rectangle is P=2L+2W, where P is the perimeter, L is the length, and W is the width. The first step is to substitute all of the data into the formula:

$$36 = 2(12) + 2W$$

Simplify by multiplying 2x12:

$$36 = 24 + 2W$$

Simplifying this further by subtracting 24 on each side, which gives:

$$36-24 = 24-24+2W$$

$$12= 2W$$

Divide by 2:

$$6 = W$$

The width is 6 cm. Remember to test this answer by substituting this value into the original formula:

$$36 = 2(12) + 2(6)$$

41. D: To find the average of a set of values, add the values together and then divide by the total number of values. In this case, include the unknown value of what Dwayne needs to score on his next test, in order to solve it.

$$\frac{78 + 92 + 83 + 97 + x}{5} = 90$$

Add the unknown value to the new average total, which is 5. Then multiply each side by 5 to simplify the equation, resulting in:

$$78 + 92 + 83 + 97 + x = 450$$

$$350 + x = 450$$

$$x = 100$$

Dwayne would need to get a perfect score of 100 in order to get an average of at least 90.

Test this answer by substituting back into the original formula.

$$\frac{78 + 92 + 83 + 97 + 100}{5} = 90$$

42. D: For an even number of total values, the *median* is calculated by finding the *mean* or average of the two middle values once all values have been arranged in ascending order from least to greatest. In this case, $(92 + 83) \div 2$ would equal the median 87.5, answer *D*.

43. C: Follow the *order of operations* in order to solve this problem. Solve the parentheses first, and then follow the remainder as usual.

$$(6 \times 4) - 9$$

This equals $24 - 9$ or 15, answer *C*.

44. D: Three girls for every two boys can be expressed as a ratio: 3:2. This can be visualized as splitting the school into 5 groups: 3 girl groups and 2 boy groups. The number of students which are in each group can be found by dividing the total number of students by 5:

650 divided by 5 equals 1 part, or 130 students per group

To find the total number of girls, multiply the number of students per group (130) by how the number of girl groups in the school (3). This equals 390, answer *D*.

45. B: To solve this correctly, keep in mind the order of operations with the mnemonic PEMDAS (Please Excuse My Dear Aunt Sally). This stands for Parentheses, Exponents, Multiplication, Division, Addition, Subtraction. Taking it step by step, solve the parentheses first:

$$4 \times 7 + (4)^2 \div 2$$

Then, apply the exponent:

$$4 \times 7 + 16 \div 2$$

Multiplication and division are both performed next:

$$28 + 8 = 36$$

46. C: Kimberley worked 4.5 hours at the rate of \$10/h and 1 hour at the rate of \$12/h. The problem states that her pay is rounded to the nearest hour, so the 4.5 hours would round up to 5 hours at the rate of \$10/h. (5h)(\$10/h)+(1h)(\$12/h)= \$50+\$12= \$62.

47. D:

$9x + x - 7 = 16 + 2x$	Combine $9x$ and x.
$10x - 7 = 16 + 2x$	
$10x - 7 + 7 = 16 + 2x + 7$	Add 7 to both sides to remove (-7).
$10x = 23 + 2x$	
$10x - 2x = 23 + 2x - 2x$	Subtract 2x from both sides to move it to the other side of the equation.
$8x = 23$	
$\dfrac{8x}{8} = \dfrac{23}{8}$	Divide by 8 to get x by itself.
$x = \dfrac{23}{8}$	

48. C: The first step is to depict each number using decimals. $\dfrac{91}{100}$ = 0.91

Multiplying both the numerator and denominator of $\dfrac{4}{5}$ by 20 makes it $\dfrac{80}{100}$ or 0.80; the closest approximation of $\dfrac{2}{3}$ would be $\dfrac{66}{100}$ or 0.66 recurring. Rearrange each expression in ascending order, as found in answer *C*.

49. B: First, calculate the difference between the larger value and the smaller value.

378 − 252 = 126

To calculate this difference as a percentage of the original value, and thus calculate the percentage *increase*, divide 126 by 252, then multiply by 100 to reach the percentage = 50%, answer *B*.

50. B: Add 3 to both sides to get $4x = 8$. Then divide both sides by 4 to get $x = 2$.

Reading Comprehension

In the Reading section, test takers will encounter passages that are roughly 250 to 350 words long, and each passage is followed by several multiple-choice questions. Test takers are given 40 questions and 40 minutes to complete the section. The passages may be poetry, fiction, and nonfiction texts from a variety of disciplines such as the humanities, sciences, social studies, and literary fiction. The questions ask students to locate information in the text and to demonstrate literal, inferential, and evaluative comprehension. Definitions of words, identifying main ideas and supporting details, and literal from nonliteral language may be addressed.

Recognizing the Main Idea

Typically, in a piece of narrative writing there are only a couple of ideas that the author is trying to convey to the reader. Be careful to understand the difference between a topic and a main idea. A topic might be "horses," but the main idea should be a complete sentence such as, "Racehorses run faster when they have a good relationship with the jockey." Here are some guidelines, tips, and tricks to follow that will help identify the main idea:

Identifying the Main Idea
The most important part of the text
Text title and pictures may reveal clues
Opening sentences and final sentences may reveal clues
Key vocabulary words that are repeatedly used may reveal clues

Topic versus the Main Idea

It is very important to know the difference between the *topic* and the *main idea* of the text. Even though these two are similar because they both present the central point of a text, they have distinctive differences. A *topic* is the subject of the text; it can usually be described in a one- to two-word phrase and appears in the simplest form. On the other hand, the *main idea* is more detailed and provides the author's central point of the text. It can be expressed through a complete sentence and is often found in the beginning, middle, or end of a paragraph. In most nonfiction books, the first sentence of the passage usually (but not always) states the main idea. Take a look at the passage below to review the *topic* versus the *main idea*.

Cheetahs

Cheetahs are one of the fastest mammals on the land, reaching up to 70 miles an hour over short distances. Even though cheetahs can run as fast as 70 miles an hour, they usually only have to run half that speed to catch up with their choice of prey. Cheetahs cannot maintain a fast pace over long periods of time because they will overheat their bodies. After a chase, cheetahs need to rest for approximately 30 minutes prior to eating or returning to any other activity.

In the example above, the *topic* of the passage is "Cheetahs" simply because that is the subject of the text. The *main idea* of the text is "Cheetahs are one of the fastest mammals on the land but can only maintain a fast pace for shorter distances." While it covers the topic, it is more detailed and refers to the text in its entirety. The text continues to provide additional details called *supporting details,* which will be discussed in the next section.

Locating Details

Supporting details of texts are defined as those elements of a text that help readers make sense of the main idea. They either qualitatively and/or quantitatively describe the main idea, strengthening the reader's understanding.

Supporting details answer questions like *who, what, where, when, why,* and *how.* Different types of supporting details include examples, facts and statistics, anecdotes, and sensory details.

Persuasive and informative texts often use supporting details. In persuasive texts, authors attempt to make readers agree with their points of view, and supporting details are often used as "selling points." If authors make a statement, they need to support the statement with evidence in order to adequately persuade readers. Informative texts use supporting details such as examples, facts, and details to inform readers. Take a look at the "Cheetahs" example again below to find examples of supporting details.

Cheetahs

Cheetahs are one of the fastest mammals on the land, reaching up to 70 miles an hour over short distances. Even though cheetahs can run as fast as 70 miles an hour, they usually only have to run half that speed to catch up with their choice of prey. Cheetahs cannot maintain a fast pace over long periods of time because they will overheat their bodies. After a chase, cheetahs need to rest for approximately 30 minutes prior to eating or returning to any other activity.

In the example above, supporting details include:

- Cheetahs reach up to 70 miles per hour over short distances.
- They usually only have to run half that speed to catch up with their prey.
- Cheetahs will overheat their bodies if they exert a high speed over longer distances.
- They need to rest for 30 minutes after a chase.

Look at the diagram below (applying the cheetah example) to help determine the hierarchy of *topic, main idea,* and *supporting details.*

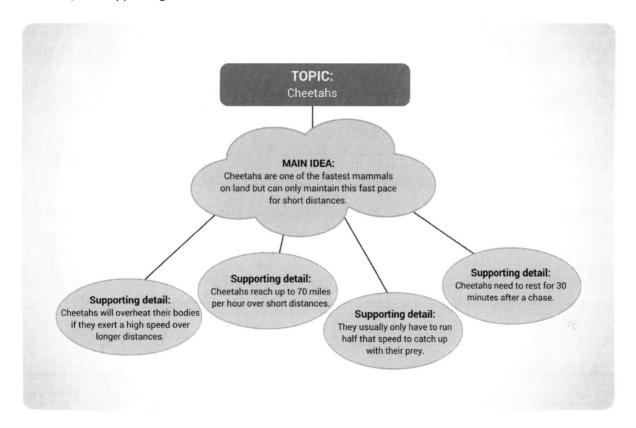

Making Inferences

Simply put, an inference is making an educated guess drawn from evidence, logic, and reasoning. The key to making inferences is identifying clues within a passage, and then using common sense to arrive at a reasonable conclusion. Consider it "reading between the lines."

One way to make an inference is to look for main topics. When doing so, pay particular attention to any titles, headlines, or opening statements made by the author. Topic sentences or repetitive ideas can be clues in gleaning inferred ideas. For example, if a passage contains the phrase *DNA testing, while some consider it infallible, is an inherently flawed technique,* the test taker can infer the rest of the passage will contain information that points to DNA testing's infallibility.

The test taker may be asked to make an inference based on prior knowledge, but may also be asked to make predictions based on new ideas. For example, the test taker may have no prior knowledge of DNA other than its genetic property to replicate. However, if the reader is given passages on the flaws of DNA testing with enough factual evidence, the test taker may arrive at the inferred conclusion that the author does not support the infallibility of DNA testing in all identification cases.

When making inferences, it is important to remember that the critical thinking process involved must be fluid and open to change. While a reader may infer an idea from a main topic, general statement, or other clues, he or she must be open to receiving new information within a particular passage. New ideas presented by an author may require the test taker to alter an inference. Similarly, when asked questions that require making an inference, it's important to read the entire test passage and all of the answer options. Often, a test taker will need to refine a general inference based on new ideas that may be presented within the test itself.

Inferences also refer to the ability to make logical assumptions based on clues from the text. People make inferences about the world around them on a daily basis but may not be aware of what they are doing. For example, a young boy may infer that it is likely cold outside if he wakes up and his bedroom is chilly or the floor is cold. While being driven somewhere on the highway and a girl notices a person at the side of the road with a parked car, that girl will likely infer that the individual is having car problems and is awaiting some assistance. Both of these are example of how inferences are used every day and the same skill can be applied to different stories and texts.

In a way, making inferences is similar to detective work by collecting evidence. Sometimes clues can be found in the pictures or visual aids (like diagrams) that accompany a story or text. For example, a story may show a picture of a school in which all children are gathered in the parking lot. Upon closer examination, careful readers might spot a fire truck parked at the side of the road and may infer that the school had a fire drill or an actual fire.

Synthesis
Synthesis also requires a reader to make inferences while reading. Inference has been addressed earlier in this guide. Review the section and take note of the required skills in making inferences.

In order to achieve synthesis and full reading comprehension, a reader must take his or her prior knowledge, the knowledge or main ideas an author presents, and fill in the gaps to reach a logical conclusion. In a testing situation, a test taker may be asked to infer ideas from a given passage, asked to choose from a set of inferences that best express a summary of what the author hints at, or arrive at a logical conclusion based on his or her inferences. This is not an easy task, but it is approachable.

While inference requires a reader to make educated guesses based on stated information, it's important that the reader does not assume too much. It's important the reader does not insert information into a passage that's not there. It's important to make an inference based solely on the presented information and to make predictions using a logical thought process.

After reviewing the earlier section on making inferences, keep the following in mind:

- Do not jump to conclusions early in the passage. Read the full text before trying to infer meaning.
- Rely on asking questions (see the above section). What is the author stating? More important, what is the author not saying? What information is missing? What conclusions can be made about that missing information, if any?
- Make an inference then apply it back to the text passage. Does the inference make sense? Is it likely an idea with which the author would agree?
- What inferences can be made from any data presented? Are these inferences sound, logical, and do they hold water?

While this is not an exhaustive list of questions related to making inferences, it should help the reader with the skill of synthesis in achieving full reading comprehension.

Deriving the Meaning of a Word or Phrase from its Context

It's common to find words that aren't familiar in writing. When you don't know a word, there are some "tricks" that can be used to find out its meaning. *Context clues* are words or phrases in a sentence or paragraph that provide hints about a word and what it means. For example, if an unknown word is attached to a noun with other surrounding words as clues, these can help you figure out the word's meaning. Consider the following example:

> After the treatment, Grandma's natural rosy cheeks looked *wan* and ghostlike.

The word we don't know is *wan.* The first clue to its meaning is in the phrase *After the treatment,* which tells us that something happened after a procedure (possibly medical). A second clue is the word *rosy,* which describes Grandma's natural cheek color that changed after the treatment. Finally, the word *ghostlike* infers that Grandma's cheeks now look white. By using the context clues in the sentence, we can figure out that the meaning of the word *wan* means *pale.*

Contrasts
Look for context clues that *contrast* the unknown word. When reading a sentence with a word we don't know, look for an opposite word or idea. Here's an example:

> Since Mary didn't cite her research sources, she lost significant points for *plagiarizing* the content of her report.

In this sentence, *plagiarizing* is the word we don't know. Notice that when Mary *didn't cite her research sources,* it resulted in her losing points for *plagiarizing the content of her report.* These contrasting ideas tell us that Mary did something wrong with the content. This makes sense because the definition of *plagiarizing* is "taking the work of someone else and passing it off as your own."

Contrasts often use words like *but, however, although,* or phrases like *on the other hand.* For example:

> The *gargantuan* television won't fit in my car, but it will cover the entire wall in the den.

The word we don't know is *gargantuan.* Notice that the television is too big to fit in a car, <u>but</u> *it will cover the entire wall in the den*. This tells us that the television is extremely large. The word *gargantuan* means *enormous.*

Synonyms
Another way to find out a word you don't know is to think of synonyms for that word. Synonyms are words with the same meaning. To do this, replace synonyms one at a time. Then read the sentence after each synonym to see if the meaning is clear. By replacing a word we don't know with a word we do know, it's easier to uncover its meaning. For example:

> Gary's clothes were *saturated* after he fell into the swimming pool.

In this sentence, we don't know the word *saturated*. To brainstorm synonyms for *saturated*, think about what happens to Gary's clothes after falling into the swimming pool. They'd be *soaked* or *wet*. These both turn out to be good synonyms to try. The actual meaning of *saturated* is "thoroughly soaked."

Antonyms

Sometimes sentences contain words or phrases that oppose each other. Opposite words are known as *antonyms*. An example of an antonym is *hot* and *cold*. For example:

> Although Mark seemed *tranquil*, you could tell he was actually nervous as he paced up and down the hall.

The word we don't know is *tranquil*. The sentence says that Mark was in fact not *tranquil.* He was *actually nervous*. The opposite of the word *nervous* is *calm*. *Calm* is the meaning of the word *tranquil*.

Explanations or Descriptions

Explanations or descriptions of other things in the sentence can also provide clues to an unfamiliar word. Take the following example:

> Golden Retrievers, Great Danes, and Pugs are the top three *breeds* competing in the dog show.

We don't know the word *breeds*. Look at the sentence for a clue. The subjects (*Golden Retrievers, Great Danes*, and *Pugs*) describe different types of dogs. This description helps uncover the meaning of the word *breeds.* The word *breeds* means "a particular type of animal."

Inferences

Inferences are clues to an unknown word that tell us its meaning. These inferences can be found within the sentence where the word appears. Or, they can be found in a sentence before the word or after the word. Look at the following example:

> The *wretched* old lady was kicked out of the restaurant. She was so mean and nasty to the waiter!

Here, we don't know the word *wretched*. The first sentence says that the *old lady was kicked out of the restaurant*, but it doesn't say why. The sentence after tells us why: *She was so mean and nasty to the waiter!* This infers that the old lady was *kicked out* because she was *so mean and nasty* or, in other words, *wretched*.

When you prepare for a vocabulary test, try reading harder materials to learn new words. If you don't know a word on the test, look for prefixes and suffixes to find out what the word means and get rid of wrong answers. If two answers both seem right, see if there are any differences between them. Then select the word that best fits. Context clues in the sentence or paragraph can also help you find the meaning of a word you don't know. By learning new words, a person can expand their knowledge. They can also improve the quality of their writing.

Determining the Author's Purpose

Authors want to capture the interest of the reader. An effective reader is attentive to an author's *position*. Authors write with intent, whether implicit or explicit. An author may hold a bias or use emotional language, which in turn creates a very clear *position.* Finding an author's *purpose* is usually easier than figuring out his or her position. An author's *purpose* of a text may be to persuade, inform, entertain, or be descriptive. Most narratives are written with the intent to entertain the reader, although some may also be informative or persuasive. When an author tries to persuade a reader, the reader must be cautious of the intent or argument. Therefore, the author keeps the persuasion lighthearted and friendly to maintain the entertainment value in narrative texts even though he or she is still trying to convince the reader of something.

An author's *purpose* will influence his or her writing style. As mentioned previously, the *purpose* can inform, entertain, or persuade a reader. If an author writes an informative text, his or her *purpose* is to educate the reader about a certain topic. Informative texts are usually nonfiction, and the author rarely states his or her opinion. The *purpose* of an informative text is also indicated by the outline of the text itself. In some cases, an informative text may have headings, subtitles, and bold key words. The *purpose* for this type of text is to educate the reader.

Entertaining texts, whether fiction or nonfiction, are meant to captivate readers' attention. Entertaining texts are usually stories that describe real or fictional people, places, or things. These narratives often use expressive language, emotions, imagery, and figurative language to captivate the readers. If readers do not want to put the entertaining text down, the author has fulfilled his or her *purpose* for this type of text.

Descriptive texts use adjectives and adverbs to describe people, places, or things to provide a clear image to the reader throughout the story. If an author fails to provide detailed descriptions, readers may find texts boring or confusing. Descriptive texts are almost always informative but can also be persuasive or entertaining pending the author's *purpose.*

Determining the Author's Attitude and Tone

Tone refers to the writer's attitude toward the subject matter. Tone is usually explained in terms of a work of fiction. For example, the tone conveys how the writer feels about their characters and the situations in which they're involved. Nonfiction writing is sometimes thought to have no tone at all, but this is incorrect.

A lot of nonfiction writing has a neutral tone, which is an extremely important tone for the writer to take. A neutral tone demonstrates that the writer is presenting a topic impartially and letting the information speak for itself. On the other hand, nonfiction writing can be just as effective and appropriate if the tone isn't neutral. For instance, take the previous examples involving seat belt use. In them, the writer mostly chooses to retain a neutral tone when presenting information. If the writer would instead include their own personal experience of losing a friend or family member in a car accident, the tone would change dramatically. The tone would no longer be neutral. Now it would show that the writer has a personal stake in the content, allowing them to interpret the information in a different way. When analyzing tone, consider what the writer is trying to achieve in the passage, and how they *create* the tone using style.

Understanding and Evaluating Opinions/Arguments

A fact is information that can be proven true. If information can be disproved, it is not a fact. For example, water freezes at or below thirty-two degrees Fahrenheit. An argument stating that water freezes at seventy degrees Fahrenheit cannot be supported by data, and is therefore not a fact. Facts tend to be associated with science, mathematics, and statistics.

Opinions are information open to debate. Opinions are often tied to subjective concepts like equality, morals, and rights. They can also be controversial. An affirmative argument for a position — such as gun control or abortion — can be just as effective as an opposing argument against it.

Stereotypes and biases are viewpoints based in opinion and held despite evidence that they are incorrect. A stereotype is a widely held belief projected onto a group, while a bias is an individual's belief. Biased people ignore evidence that contradicts their position while offering as proof any evidence that supports it. Those who stereotype tend to make assumptions based on what others have told them and usually have little firsthand experience with the group or item in question.

When it comes to authors' writings, readers should always identify a position or stance. No matter how objective a text may seem, assume the author has preconceived beliefs. Reduce the likelihood of accepting an invalid argument, by looking for multiple articles on the topic, including those with varying opinions. If several opinions point in the same direction, and are backed by reputable peer-reviewed sources, it's more likely the author has a valid argument. Positions that run contrary to widely held beliefs and existing data should invite scrutiny. There are exceptions to the rule, so be a careful consumer of information.

Making Predictions Based on Information in the Passage

An active reader uses prior knowledge while reading to make accurate predictions. Prior knowledge is best utilized when readers make links between the current text, previously read texts, and life experiences. Some texts use suspense and foreshadowing to captivate readers. For example, an intriguing aspect of murder mysteries is that the reader is never sure of the culprit until the author reveals the individual's identity. Authors often build suspense, and add depth and meaning to a work by leaving clues to provide hints or predict future events in the story; this is called foreshadowing. While some instances of foreshadowing are subtle, others are quite obvious.

Another way to read actively is to identify examples of inference within text. Authors employ literary devices such as tone, characterization, and theme to engage the audience by showing details of the story instead of merely telling them. For example, if an author said *Bob is selfish*, there's little left to infer. If the author said, *Bob cheated on his test, ignored his mom's calls, and parked illegally*, the reader can infer Bob is selfish. Authors also make implications through character dialogue, thoughts, effects on others, actions, and looks. Like in life, readers must assemble all the clues to form a complete picture.

Active readers should also draw conclusions. A conclusion should be based only on the text details, not personal experiences. This means the reader should first determine the author's intent. Identify the author's viewpoint and connect relevant evidence to support it. Readers may then move to the most important step: deciding whether to agree and whether they are correct. Always read cautiously and critically. Interact with text and record reactions in the margins. These active reading skills help determine not only what the author thinks, but what the reader thinks.

Practice Questions

Questions 1 – 5 are based on the following passage.

George Washington emerged out of the American Revolution as an unlikely champion of liberty. On June 14, 1775, the Second Continental Congress created the Continental Army, and John Adams, serving in the Congress, nominated Washington to be its first commander. Washington fought under the British during the French and Indian War, and his experience and prestige proved instrumental to the American war effort. Washington provided invaluable leadership, training, and strategy during the Revolutionary War. He emerged from the war as the embodiment of liberty and freedom from tyranny.

After vanquishing the heavily favored British forces, Washington could have pronounced himself as the autocratic leader of the former colonies without any opposition, but he famously refused and returned to his Mount Vernon plantation. His restraint proved his commitment to the fledgling state's republicanism. Washington was later unanimously elected as the first American president. But it is Washington's farewell address that cemented his legacy as a visionary worthy of study.

In 1796, President Washington issued his farewell address by public letter. Washington enlisted his good friend, Alexander Hamilton, in drafting his most famous address. The letter expressed Washington's faith in the Constitution and rule of law. He encouraged his fellow Americans to put aside partisan differences and establish a national union. Washington warned Americans against meddling in foreign affairs and entering military alliances. Additionally, he stated his opposition to national political parties, which he considered partisan and counterproductive.

Americans would be wise to remember Washington's farewell, especially during presidential elections when politics hits a fever pitch. They might want to question the political institutions that were not planned by the Founding Fathers, such as the nomination process and political parties themselves.

1. Which of the following statements is based on the information in the passage above?
   a. George Washington's background as a wealthy landholder directly led to his faith in equality, liberty, and democracy.
   b. George Washington would have opposed America's involvement in the Second World War.
   c. George Washington would not have been able to write as great a farewell address without the assistance of Alexander Hamilton.
   d. George Washington would probably not approve of modern political parties.

2. What is the purpose of this passage?
   a. To inform American voters about a Founding Father's sage advice on a contemporary issue and explain its applicability to modern times
   b. To introduce George Washington to readers as a historical figure worthy of study
   c. To note that George Washington was more than a famous military hero
   d. To convince readers that George Washington is a hero of republicanism and liberty

3. What is the tone of the passage?
   a. Informative
   b. Excited
   c. Bitter
   d. Comic

4. What does the word *meddling* mean in paragraph 3?
   a. Supporting
   b. Speaking against
   c. Interfering
   d. Gathering

5. According to the passage, what did George Washington do when he was offered a role as leader of the former colonies?
   a. He refused the offer.
   b. He accepted the offer.
   c. He became angry at the offer.
   d. He accepted the offer then regretted it later.

Questions 6 – 10 are based on the following passage.

Christopher Columbus is often credited with discovering America. This is incorrect. First, it is impossible to "discover" something where people already live; however, Christopher Columbus did explore places in the New World that were previously untouched by Europe, so the term "explorer" would be more accurate. Another correction must be made, as well: Christopher Columbus was not the first European explorer to reach the present day Americas! Rather, it was Leif Erikson who first came to the New World and contacted the natives, nearly five hundred years before Christopher Columbus.

Leif Erikson, the son of Erik the Red (a famous Viking outlaw and explorer in his own right), was born in either 970 or 980, depending on which historian you seek. His own family, though, did not raise Leif, which was a Viking tradition. Instead, one of Erik's prisoners taught Leif reading and writing, languages, sailing, and weaponry. At age 12, Leif was considered a man and returned to his family. He killed a man during a dispute shortly after his return, and the council banished the Erikson clan to Greenland.

In 999, Leif left Greenland and traveled to Norway where he would serve as a guard to King Olaf Tryggvason. It was there that he became a convert to Christianity. Leif later tried to return home with the intention of taking supplies and spreading Christianity to Greenland, however his ship was blown off course and he arrived in a strange new land: present day Newfoundland, Canada.

When he finally returned to his adopted homeland Greenland, Leif consulted with a merchant who had also seen the shores of this previously unknown land we now know as Canada. The son of the legendary Viking explorer then gathered a crew of 35 men and set sail. Leif became the first European to touch foot in the New World as he explored present-day Baffin Island and Labrador, Canada. His crew called the land Vinland since it was plentiful with grapes.

During their time in present-day Newfoundland, Leif's expedition made contact with the natives whom they referred to as Skraelings (which translates to "wretched ones" in Norse). There are several secondhand accounts of their meetings. Some contemporaries described trade between the peoples. Other accounts describe clashes where the Skraelings defeated the Viking explorers with long spears, while still others claim the Vikings dominated the natives. Regardless of the circumstances, it seems that the Vikings made contact of some kind. This happened around 1000, nearly five hundred years before Columbus famously sailed the ocean blue.

Eventually, in 1003, Leif set sail for home and arrived at Greenland with a ship full of timber.

In 1020, seventeen years later, the legendary Viking died. Many believe that Leif Erikson should receive more credit for his contributions in exploring the New World.

6. Which of the following best describes how the author generally presents the information?
   a. Chronological order
   b. Comparison-contrast
   c. Cause-effect
   d. Conclusion-premises

7. Which of the following is an opinion, rather than historical fact, expressed by the author?
   a. Leif Erikson was definitely the son of Erik the Red; however, historians debate the year of his birth.
   b. Leif Erikson's crew called the land Vinland since it was plentiful with grapes.
   c. Leif Erikson deserves more credit for his contributions in exploring the New World.
   d. Leif Erikson explored the Americas nearly five hundred years before Christopher Columbus.

8. Which of the following most accurately describes the author's main conclusion?
   a. Leif Erikson is a legendary Viking explorer.
   b. Leif Erikson deserves more credit for exploring America hundreds of years before Columbus.
   c. Spreading Christianity motivated Leif Erikson's expeditions more than any other factor.
   d. Leif Erikson contacted the natives nearly five hundred years before Columbus.

9. Which of the following best describes the author's intent in the passage?
   a. To entertain
   b. To inform
   c. To alert
   d. To suggest

10. Which of the following can be logically inferred from the passage?
    a. The Vikings disliked exploring the New World.
    b. Leif Erikson's banishment from Iceland led to his exploration of present-day Canada.
    c. Leif Erikson never shared his stories of exploration with the King of Norway.
    d. Historians have difficulty definitively pinpointing events in the Vikings' history.
    The next five questions are based on the chart following a brief introduction to the topic.

Questions 11 – 15 are based on the following passage.

Smoking is Terrible

Smoking tobacco products is terribly destructive. A single cigarette contains over 4,000 chemicals, including 43 known carcinogens and 400 deadly toxins. Some of the most dangerous ingredients include tar, carbon monoxide, formaldehyde, ammonia, arsenic, and DDT. Smoking can cause numerous types of cancer including throat, mouth, nasal cavity, esophagus, stomach, pancreas, kidney, bladder, and cervical.

Cigarettes contain a drug called nicotine, one of the most addictive substances known to man. Addiction is defined as a compulsion to seek the substance despite negative consequences. According to the National Institute of Drug Abuse, nearly 35 million smokers expressed a desire to quit smoking in 2015; however, more than 85 percent of those addicts will not achieve their goal. Almost all smokers regret picking up that first cigarette. You would be wise to learn from their mistake if you have not yet started smoking.

According to the U.S. Department of Health and Human Services, 16 million people in the United States presently suffer from a smoking-related condition and nearly nine million suffer from a serious smoking-related illness. According to the Centers for Disease Control and Prevention (CDC), tobacco products cause nearly six million deaths per year. This number is projected to rise to over eight million deaths by 2030. Smokers, on average, die ten years earlier than their nonsmoking peers.

In the United States, local, state, and federal governments typically tax tobacco products, which leads to high prices. Nicotine addicts sometimes pay more for a pack of cigarettes than for a few gallons of gas. Additionally, smokers tend to stink. The smell of smoke is all-consuming and creates a pervasive nastiness. Smokers also risk staining their teeth and fingers with yellow residue from the tar.

Smoking is deadly, expensive, and socially unappealing. Clearly, smoking is not worth the risks.

11. Which of the following statements most accurately summarizes the passage?
    a. Tobacco is less healthy than many alternatives.
    b. Tobacco is deadly, expensive, and socially unappealing, and smokers would be much better off kicking the addiction.
    c. In the United States, local, state, and federal governments typically tax tobacco products, which leads to high prices.
    d. Tobacco products shorten smokers' lives by ten years and kill more than six million people per year.

12. The author would be most likely to agree with which of the following statements?
    a. Smokers should only quit cold turkey and avoid all nicotine cessation devices.
    b. Other substances are more addictive than tobacco.
    c. Smokers should quit for whatever reason that gets them to stop smoking.
    d. People who want to continue smoking should advocate for a reduction in tobacco product taxes.

13. Which of the following is the author's opinion?
    a. According to the Centers for Disease Control and Prevention (CDC), tobacco products cause nearly six million deaths per year.
    b. Nicotine addicts sometimes pay more for a pack of cigarettes than a few gallons of gas.
    c. They also risk staining their teeth and fingers with yellow residue from the tar.
    d. Additionally, smokers tend to stink. The smell of smoke is all-consuming and creates a pervasive nastiness.

14. What is the tone of this passage?
   a. Objective
   b. Cautionary
   c. Philosophical
   d. Admiring

15. What does the word *pervasive* mean in paragraph 4?
   a. Pleasantly appealing
   b. A floral scent
   c. To convince someone
   d. All over the place

Questions 16 – 20 are based on the following passage.

The Myth of Head Heat Loss

It has recently been brought to my attention that most people believe that 75% of your body heat is lost through your head. I had certainly heard this before, and am not going to attempt to say I didn't believe it when I first heard it. It is natural to be gullible to anything said with enough authority. But the "fact" that the majority of your body heat is lost through your head is a lie.

Let me explain. Heat loss is proportional to surface area exposed. An elephant loses a great deal more heat than an anteater, because it has a much greater surface area than an anteater. Each cell has mitochondria that produce energy in the form of heat, and it takes a lot more energy to run an elephant than an anteater.

So, each part of your body loses its proportional amount of heat in accordance with its surface area. The human torso probably loses the most heat, though the legs lose a significant amount as well. Some people have asked, "Why does it feel so much warmer when you cover your head than when you don't?" Well, that's because your head, because it is not clothed, is losing a lot of heat while the clothing on the rest of your body provides insulation. If you went outside with a hat and pants but no shirt, not only would you look silly, but your heat loss would be significantly greater because so much more of you would be exposed. So, if given the choice to cover your chest or your head in the cold, choose the chest. It could save your life.

16. Why does the author compare elephants and anteaters?
   a. To express an opinion.
   b. To give an example that helps clarify the main point.
   c. To show the differences between them.
   d. To persuade why one is better than the other.

17. Which of the following best describes the tone of the passage?
   a. Harsh
   b. Angry
   c. Casual
   d. Indifferent

18. The author appeals to which branch of rhetoric to prove their case?
    a. Factual evidence
    b. Emotion
    c. Ethics and morals
    d. Author qualification

19. What does the word *gullible* mean in paragraph 1?
    a. To be angry toward
    b. To distrust something
    c. To believe something easily
    d. To be happy toward

20. What is the main idea of the passage?
    a. To debunk the myth that heat loss comes mostly from the head.
    b. To prove that you have to have a hat to survive in the cold.
    c. To persuade the audience that anteaters are better than elephants.
    d. To convince the audience that heat loss comes mostly from the head.

This article discusses the famous poet and playwright William Shakespeare. Read it and answer questions 21 – 25.

People who argue that William Shakespeare is not responsible for the plays attributed to his name are known as anti-Stratfordians (from the name of Shakespeare's birthplace, Stratford-upon-Avon). The most common anti-Stratfordian claim is that William Shakespeare simply was not educated enough or from a high enough social class to have written plays overflowing with references to such a wide range of subjects like history, the classics, religion, and international culture. William Shakespeare was the son of a glove-maker, he only had a basic grade school education, and he never set foot outside of England—so how could he have produced plays of such sophistication and imagination? How could he have written in such detail about historical figures and events, or about different cultures and locations around Europe? According to anti-Stratfordians, the depth of knowledge contained in Shakespeare's plays suggests a well-traveled writer from a wealthy background with a university education, not a countryside writer like Shakespeare. But in fact, there is not much substance to such speculation, and most anti-Stratfordian arguments can be refuted with a little background about Shakespeare's time and upbringing.

First of all, those who doubt Shakespeare's authorship often point to his common birth and brief education as stumbling blocks to his writerly genius. Although it is true that Shakespeare did not come from a noble class, his father was a very *successful* glove-maker and his mother was from a very wealthy land owning family—so while Shakespeare may have had a country upbringing, he was certainly from a well-off family and would have been educated accordingly. Also, even though he did not attend university, grade school education in Shakespeare's time was actually quite rigorous and exposed students to classic drama through writers like Seneca and Ovid. It is not unreasonable to believe that Shakespeare received a very solid foundation in poetry and literature from his early schooling.

Next, anti-Stratfordians tend to question how Shakespeare could write so extensively about countries and cultures he had never visited before (for instance, several of his most famous works like *Romeo and Juliet* and *The Merchant of Venice* were set in Italy, on the opposite side of Europe!). But again, this criticism does not hold up under scrutiny. For one thing, Shakespeare was living in London, a bustling metropolis of international trade, the most populous city in England, and a political and cultural hub of Europe. In the daily crowds of people, Shakespeare would certainly have been able to meet travelers from other countries and hear firsthand accounts of life in their home country. And, in addition to the influx of information from world travelers, this was also the age of the printing press, a jump in technology that made it possible to print and circulate books much more easily than in the past. This also allowed for a freer flow of information across different countries, allowing people to read about life and ideas from throughout Europe. One needn't travel the continent in order to learn and write about its culture.

21. Which sentence contains the author's thesis?

a. People who argue that William Shakespeare is not responsible for the plays attributed to his name are known as anti-Stratfordians.

b. But in fact, there is not much substance to such speculation, and most anti-Stratfordian arguments can be refuted with a little background about Shakespeare's time and upbringing.

c. It is not unreasonable to believe that Shakespeare received a very solid foundation in poetry and literature from his early schooling.

d. Next, anti-Stratfordians tend to question how Shakespeare could write so extensively about countries and cultures he had never visited before.

22. In the first paragraph, "How could he have written in such detail about historical figures and events, or about different cultures and locations around Europe?" is an example of which of the following?

a. Hyperbole
b. Onomatopoeia
c. Rhetorical question
d. Appeal to authority

23. How does the author respond to the claim that Shakespeare was not well-educated because he did not attend university?

a. By insisting upon Shakespeare's natural genius.
b. By explaining grade school curriculum in Shakespeare's time.
c. By comparing Shakespeare with other uneducated writers of his time.
d. By pointing out that Shakespeare's wealthy parents probably paid for private tutors.

24. The word "bustling" in the third paragraph most nearly means which of the following?

a. Busy
b. Foreign
c. Expensive
d. Undeveloped

25. According to the passage, what did Shakespeare's father do to make a living?

a. He was a king's guard.
b. He acted in plays.
c. He was a glove-maker.
d. He was a cobbler.

Questions 26 – 30 are based on the following passage.

Do you want to vacation at a Caribbean island destination? We chose to go to St. Lucia, and it was the best vacation we ever had. We lounged in crystal blue waters, swam with dolphins, and enjoyed a family-friendly resort and activities. One of the activities we did was free diving in the ocean. We put our snorkels on, waded into the ocean, and swam down to the ocean floor. The water was clear all the way down—the greens and blues were so beautiful. We saw a stingray, some conches, and a Caribbean Reef Shark. The shark was so scary, I came up to the surface after that! But the rest of the day was spent lying on the beach, getting massages, and watching other kids play with a Frisbee in front of the water.

Towards the end of our vacation, I was reluctant to go home. We started to pack our things, and then I realized I wanted to take one more walk with my mom and dad. Our resort was between the ocean and some mountains, so we decided to hike up a mountain and enjoy the view of the beach from way up high! We trekked for what seemed like miles, observing the vegetation along the way; it was so lush with reds and greens and blues. Finally, we got up to the top of the mountain and observed the wonderful ocean that stretched on for hundreds of miles. On our way back down, I felt totally at peace to be leaving the island, although I would miss it very much and would want to visit the island again soon. You should visit St. Lucia, or pick another island in the Caribbean! Every island offers a unique and dazzling vacation destination.

26. What Island did the family stay on?
    a. St. Lucia
    b. Barbados
    c. Antigua
    d. Saint Kitts

27. What is/are the supporting detail(s) of this passage?
    a. Cruising to the Caribbean
    b. Local events
    c. Family activities
    d. All of the above

28. What was the last activity the speaker did?
    a. Swam with the sharks
    b. Went for a hike up a mountain
    c. Lounged on the beach
    d. Surfed in the waves

29. Which of the following is the best definition for the word *trekked* in the second paragraph?
    a. Walked
    b. Ran
    c. Swam
    d. Sang

30. Which of the following words best describes the author's attitude toward the topic?
    a. Worried
    b. Resigned
    c. Objective
    d. Enthusiastic

Questions 31 – 35 are based on the following passage.

Even though the rain can put a damper on the day, it can be helpful and fun, too. For one, the rain helps plants grow. Without rain, grass, flowers, and trees would be deprived of vital nutrients they need to develop. It's like how humans need water to survive; plants also need water to survive and flourish and keep that wonderful green color instead of turning brown.

Not only does the rain help plants grow, but on days where there are brief spurts of sunshine, rainbows can appear. The rain reflects and refracts the light, creating beautiful rainbows in the sky. One time I was on a trip with my brother across the United States. Before the trip, we said that we wanted to see a rainbow in every state we went through. We ended up driving through eleven states, and guess what? We saw fifteen rainbows, at least one in each state. What an incredible trip!

Finally, puddle jumping is another fun activity that can be done in or after the rain. Whenever there are heavy thunder storms, I always look forward to when the storm lifts. I usually go outside right after, because there are a lot of families in my neighborhood, and I love to watch all the children jump, skip, and splash in the puddles. The bigger kids create huge torrents of water and the smaller kids create little splashes. Thinking about all the positive things rain brings to us, I know that rain can be helpful and fun.

31. What is the *cause* in this passage?
    a. Plants growing
    b. Rainbows
    c. Puddle jumping
    d. Rain

32. In the following sentence, the author is using what literary device regarding the grass, flowers, and trees?
    "Without rain, grass, flowers, and trees would be deprived of vital nutrients they need to develop."

    a. Comparing
    b. Contrasting
    c. Describing
    d. Transitioning

33. In the same sentence from above, what is most likely the meaning of *vital?*
    a. Energetic
    b. Truthful
    c. Necessary
    d. Dangerous

34. What is an *effect* in this passage?
    a. Rain
    b. Brief spurts of sunshine
    c. Rainbows
    d. Weather

35. What kind of evidence does the author use most in this passage?
    a. Interviews
    b. Personal testimonies
    c. Journal articles
    d. Statistics

Sylvia's father was a beekeeper and Sylvia loved watching him take care of bees. When he was gone to work, Sylvia would stealthily try to find bees in her garden and pretend like she was her father on a magnificent mission to save all the bees she came into contact with. She really just wanted to be helpful. So, she started to pick out all the bees (she wasn't afraid of the stingers, though she had been stung several times in the past), and put them in jars in her house so that they could all be safe from harm.

One day Sylvia's mother walked into her bedroom and noticed that Sylvia had a large container that her mother had never seen before. When Sylvia's mother opened the container, a swarm of bees flew out and started to buzz around her mother's head! Sylvia's mother screamed and ran out of the room, her face scrunched in terror. Sylvia was outside playing, and when she saw her mother run out of the house, Sylvia knew immediately what had happened. Her mother found the bee jar! She quickly helped her mother swat away the bees and told her mother that she just wanted to help the bees stay safe from the outside harms that could come to them. "Sylvia," her mother said, "Do you feel afraid when you are outside?" "No," Sylvia replied. "I feel safe, and I have lots of fun out here." "Well," her mother said, "the bees are just like you! They love the sunlight, and the flowers are so important to them they fly around them all day and never get tired. Leave the bees outside, and they will thank you for it." Sylvia laughed at her own thoughts and knew that the bees would be safer outside, away from her terrified mother and into the hands of nature.

36. What does the word *stealthily* mean in paragraph 1?
    a. Hurriedly
    b. Begrudgingly
    c. Confidently
    d. Secretly

37. What point of view is the story written in?
    a. First person
    b. Second person
    c. Third person
    d. No person

38. According to the passage, why did Sylvia want to keep the bees inside a jar?
    a. She wanted to conduct a science experiment with them.
    b. She wanted to keep them away from harm.
    c. She wanted to bring them as a gift to her father.
    d. She wanted to use them to scare her mother.

39. How is this passage organized?
    a. Chronological
    b. Cause and effect
    c. Problem to solution
    d. Sequential

40. What would you say is the theme of the passage?
    a. Loss/Grief
    b. Friendship
    c. Freedom
    d. Suffering

Answer Explanations

1. D: Although Washington is from a wealthy background, the passage does not say that his wealth led to his republican ideals, so Choice A is not supported. Choice B also does not follow from the passage. Washington's warning against meddling in foreign affairs does not mean that he would oppose wars of every kind, so Choice B is incorrect. Choice C is also unjustified since the author does not indicate that Alexander Hamilton's assistance was absolutely necessary. Choice D is correct because the farewell address clearly opposes political parties and partisanship. The author then notes that presidential elections often hit a fever pitch of partisanship. Thus, it is follows that George Washington would not approve of modern political parties and their involvement in presidential elections.

2. A: The author finishes the passage by applying Washington's farewell address to modern politics, so the purpose probably includes this application. Choice B is incorrect because George Washington is already a well-established historical figure; furthermore, the passage does not seek to introduce him. Choice C is incorrect because the author is not fighting a common perception that Washington was merely a military hero. Choice D is incorrect because the author is not convincing readers. Persuasion does not correspond to the passage. Choice A states the primary purpose.

3. A: The tone in this passage is informative. Choice B, excited, is incorrect, because there are not many word choices used that would indicate excitement from the author. Choice C, bitter, is incorrect. Although the author does make a suggestion in the last paragraph to Americans, the statement is not necessarily bitter, but based on the preceding information. Choice D, comic, is incorrect, as the author does not try to make the audience laugh, nor do they make light of the situation in any way.

4. C: Interfering. Meddling means to interfere in something. Choice A is incorrect. One helpful thing would be to use the word in the sentence: "Washington warned Americans against 'supporting' in foreign affairs" does not make that much sense, so we can mark it off. Choice B, speaking against, is incorrect. This phrase would make sense in the sentence, but it goes against the meaning that is intended. George Washington warned against interference in foreign affairs, not speaking *against* foreign affairs. Finally, gathering is also incorrect, because "gathering in foreign affairs" does not sound quite right. Interfering is the best choice for this question.

5. D: When Washington was offered a role as leader of the former colonies, he refused the offer. This is explained in the first sentence of the second paragraph. All of the other answer choices are incorrect and not mentioned in the passage.

6. D: The passage does not proceed in chronological order since it begins by pointing out Leif Erikson's explorations in America so Choice A does not work. Although the author compares and contrasts Erikson with Christopher Columbus, this is not the main way the information is presented; therefore, Choice B does not work. Neither does Choice C because there is no mention of or reference to cause and effect in the passage. However, the passage does offer a conclusion (Leif Erikson deserves more credit) and premises (first European to set foot in the New World and first to contact the natives) to substantiate Erikson's historical importance. Thus, Choice D is correct.

7. C: Choice A is incorrect because it describes facts: Leif Erikson was the son of Erik the Red and historians debate Leif's date of birth. These are not opinions. Choice B is incorrect; that Erikson called the land Vinland is a verifiable fact as is Choice D because he did contact the natives almost 500 years before Columbus. Choice C is the correct answer because it is the author's opinion that Erikson deserves more credit. That, in fact, is his conclusion in the piece, but another person could argue that Columbus or another explorer deserves more credit for opening up the New World to exploration. Rather than being an incontrovertible fact, it is a subjective value claim.

8. B: Choice *A* is incorrect because the author aims to go beyond describing Erikson as a mere legendary Viking. Choice *C* is incorrect because the author does not focus on Erikson's motivations, let alone name the spreading of Christianity as his primary objective. Choice *D* is incorrect because it is a premise that Erikson contacted the natives 500 years before Columbus, which is simply a part of supporting the author's conclusion. Choice *B* is correct because, as stated in the previous answer, it accurately identifies the author's statement that Erikson deserves more credit than he has received for being the first European to explore the New World.

9. B: Choice *A* is incorrect because the author is not in any way trying to entertain the reader. Choice *D* is incorrect certainly trying to alert the readers (make them aware) of Leif Erikson's underappreciated and unheralded accomplishments, the nature of the writing does not indicate the author would be satisfied with the reader merely knowing of Erikson's exploration (Choice *C*). Rather, the author would want the reader to be informed about it, which is more substantial (Choice *B*).

10. D: Choice *A* is incorrect because the author never addresses the Vikings' state of mind or emotions. Choice *B* is incorrect because the author does not elaborate on Erikson's exile and whether he would have become an explorer if not for his banishment. Choice *C* is incorrect because there is not enough information to support this premise. It is unclear whether Erikson informed the King of Norway of his finding. Although it is true that the King did not send a follow-up expedition, he could have simply chosen not to expend the resources after receiving Erikson's news. It is not possible to logically infer whether Erikson told him. Choice *D* is correct because there are two examples—Leif Erikson's date of birth and what happened during the encounter with the natives—of historians having trouble pinning down important dates in Viking history.

11. B: The author is clearly opposed to tobacco. He cites disease and deaths associated with smoking. He points to the monetary expense and aesthetic costs. Choice *A* is incorrect because alternatives to smoking are not even addressed in the passage. Choice *C* is incorrect because it does not summarize the passage but rather is just a premise. Choice *D* is incorrect because, while these statistics are a premise in the argument, they do not represent a summary of the piece. Choice *B* is the correct answer because it states the three critiques offered against tobacco and expresses the author's conclusion.

12. C: We are looking for something the author would agree with, so it will almost certainly be anti-smoking or an argument in favor of quitting smoking. Choice *A* is incorrect because the author does not speak against means of cessation. Choice *B* is incorrect because the author does not reference other substances, but does speak of how addictive nicotine, a drug in tobacco, is. Choice *D* is incorrect because the author certainly would not encourage reducing taxes to encourage a reduction of smoking costs, thereby helping smokers to continue the habit. Choice *C* is correct because the author is definitely attempting to persuade smokers to quit smoking.

13. D: Here, we are looking for an opinion of the author's rather than a fact or statistic. Choice *A* is incorrect because quoting statistics from the Centers of Disease Control and Prevention is stating facts, not opinions. Choice *B* is incorrect because it expresses the fact that cigarettes sometimes cost more than a few gallons of gas. It would be an opinion if the author said that cigarettes were not affordable. Choice *C* is incorrect because yellow stains are a known possible adverse effect of smoking. Choice *D* is correct as an opinion because smell is subjective. Some people might like the smell of smoke, they might not have working olfactory senses, and/or some people might not find the smell of smoke akin to "pervasive nastiness," so this is the expression of an opinion. Thus, Choice *D* is the correct answer.

14. B: The passage is cautionary, because the author warns about the hazards of smoking and uses the second-person "you" to offer suggestions, like "You would be wise to learn from their mistake." Choice *A*, objective, means that the passage would be totally without persuasion or suggestions, so this answer choice is incorrect. Choice *C*, philosophical, is incorrect, because this is a down-to-earth passage that presents facts and gives suggestions based on those facts, and there are no philosophical underpinnings here. Finally, Choice *D* is incorrect. The passage is opposite of admiring towards the subject of smoking.

15. D: The word *pervasive* means "all over the place." The passage says that "The smell of smoke is all-consuming and creates a *pervasive* nastiness," which means a smell that is *everywhere* or *all over*. Choices *A* and *B*, pleasantly appealing and a floral scent, are too pleasant for the context of the passage. Choice *D* doesn't make sense in the sentence, as "to convince someone" wouldn't really describe the word *nastiness* like pervasive does.

16. B: Choice *B* is correct because the author is trying to demonstrate the main idea, which is that heat loss is proportional to surface area, and so they compare two animals with different surface areas to clarify the main point. Choice *A* is incorrect because the author uses elephants and anteaters to prove a point, that heat loss is proportional to surface area, not to express an opinion. Choice *C* is incorrect because though the author does use them to show differences, they do so in order to give examples that prove the above points, so Choice *C* is not the best answer. Choice *D* is incorrect because there is no language to indicate favoritism between the two animals.

17. C: Because of the way that the author addresses the reader, and also the colloquial language that the author uses (i.e., "let me explain," "so," "well," didn't," "you would look silly," etc.), *C* is the best answer because it has a much more casual tone than the usual informative article. *Choice A* may be a tempting choice because the author says the "fact" that most of one's heat is lost through their head is a "lie," and that someone who does not wear a shirt in the cold looks silly, but it only happens twice within all the diction of the passage and it does not give an overall tone of harshness. *B* is incorrect because again, while not necessarily nice, the language does not carry an angry charge. The author is clearly not indifferent to the subject because of the passionate language that they use, so *D* is incorrect.

18. A: The author gives logical examples and reasons in order to prove that most of one's heat is not lost through their head, therefore *A* is correct. *B* is incorrect because there is not much emotionally charged language in this selection, and even the small amount present is greatly outnumbered by the facts and evidence. *C* is incorrect because there is no mention of ethics or morals in this selection. *D* is incorrect because the author never qualifies himself as someone who has the authority to be writing on this topic.

19. C: *Gullible* means to believe something easily. The other answer choices could fit easily within the context of the passage: you can be angry toward, distrustful toward, or happy toward authority. For this answer choice and the surrounding context, however, the author talks about a myth that people believe easily, so *gullible* would be the word that fits best in this context.

20. A: To debunk the myth that heat loss comes mostly from the head. The whole passage is dedicated to debunking the head heat loss myth. The passage says that "each part of your body loses its proportional amount of heat in accordance with its surface area," which means an area such as the chest would lose more heat than the head because it's bigger. The other answer choices are incorrect.

21. B: But in fact, there is not much substance to such speculation, and most anti-Stratfordian arguments can be refuted with a little background about Shakespeare's time and upbringing. The thesis is a statement that contains the author's topic and main idea. The main purpose of this article is to use historical evidence to provide counterarguments to anti-Stratfordians. Choice A is simply a definition; Choice C is a supporting detail, not a main idea; and Choice D represents an idea of anti-Stratfordians, not the author's opinion.

22. C: Rhetorical question. This requires readers to be familiar with different types of rhetorical devices. A rhetorical question is a question that is asked not to obtain an answer but to encourage readers to more deeply consider an issue.

23. B: By explaining grade school curriculum in Shakespeare's time. This question asks readers to refer to the organizational structure of the article and demonstrate understanding of how the author provides details to support their argument. This particular detail can be found in the second paragraph: "even though he did not attend university, grade school education in Shakespeare's time was actually quite rigorous."

24. A: Busy. This is a vocabulary question that can be answered using context clues. Other sentences in the paragraph describe London as "the most populous city in England" filled with "crowds of people," giving an image of a busy city full of people. Choice B is incorrect because London was in Shakespeare's home country, not a foreign one. Choice C is not mentioned in the passage. Choice D is not a good answer choice because the passage describes how London was a popular and important city, probably not an underdeveloped one.

25. C: Shakespeare's father was a glove-maker. The passage states this fact in paragraph two, where it says "his father was a very successful glove-maker." The other answer choices are incorrect.

26. A: St Lucia. The author mentions St. Lucia a couple times throughout the passage. The other answer choices are incorrect.

27. C: Family resorts and activities. Remember that supporting details help readers find out the main idea by answering questions like *who, what, where, when, why,* and *how.* In this question, cruises and local events are not talked about in the passage. However, family resorts and activities are talked about.

28. B: The last activity the speaker did was went for a hike up a mountain. We know this because the speaker "wanted to take one more walk" before the family left. The speaker did do Choices A and C, swam with the sharks and lounged on the beach, but those weren't the last activities the speaker did. The speaker never said anything about surfing in the waves, so Choice D is incorrect.

29. A: To trek means to hike or walk, so Choice A is the best answer here. Choices B, C, and D, ran, swam, and sang, are incorrect.

30. D: The author's attitude towards the topic is enthusiastic. We see the author's enthusiasm through the word choice such as *best vacation, enjoyed, beautiful,* and *peace.* We also see the author using multiple exclamation marks, which denotes excitement. Therefore, our best answer is Choice D. The author doesn't demonstrate any worry or resignation, except maybe a bit in the part where they have to go home soon, but the enthusiasm overrides these feelings in the rest of the passage. Choice C, objective, means to be fair and based in fact, and the author is far too enthusiastic toward St. Lucia, which creates some bias towards the topic.

31. D: Rain. Rain is the cause in this passage because it is why something happened. The effects are plants growing, rainbows, and puddle jumping.

32. A: Comparing. The author is comparing the plants, trees, and flowers. The author is showing how these things react the same to rain. They all get important nutrients from rain. If the author described the differences, then it would be contrasting, Choice *B*.

33. C: Necessary. *Vital* can mean different things depending on the context or how it is used. But in this sentence, the word *vital* means necessary. The word *vital* means full of life and energy. Choices *A* and *B*, *energetic* and *truthful,* do not make sense. Choice *D, dangerous,* is almost an antonym for the word we are looking for since the sentence says the nutrients are needed for growing. Something needed would not be dangerous. The best context clue is that it says the vital nutrients are needed, which tells us they are necessary.

34. C: Rainbows. This passage mentions several effects. Effects are the outcome of a certain cause. Remember that the cause here is rain, so Choice *A* is incorrect. Since the cause is rain, Choice *B*—brief spurts of sunshine—doesn't make sense because rain doesn't *cause* brief spurts of sunshine. Choice *C* makes the most sense because the effects of the rain in the passage are plants growing, rainbows, and puddle jumping. Lastly, Choice *D*, weather, is not an effect of rain but describes rain in a general sense.

35. B: The author uses personal testimonies in this passage. We see this in the second and third paragraphs. The first time the author gives a personal testimony is when they talk about going on a trip across the United States and seeing all the rainbows. The second personal testimony we see is when the author goes outside after a storm to watch everyone play in the puddles. The other answer choices are not represented in the passage.

36. D: *Stealthily* means secretly, Choice *D*. Given the context of the passage, we probably can assume that Sylvia was trying her best to be *secretive*, since she was gathering bees while her father was away at work. Hurriedly might fit, Choice *A*, but it is not the best answer. Begrudgingly ,Choice *B*, is incorrect, because if Sylvia was begrudging, or resentful, that she had to gather bees, she probably wouldn't have done it. Finally, Choice *C*, confidently, although it could fit in this context, is not the best choice for this definition.

37. C: The story is written in third-person, which tells the story using *he, she, they*, etc. First person narrative is used when the narrator is an "I" in the story, so it'll use language such as "I," "we," etc. There are no instances of "I" or "we" in the story, so Choice *A* is incorrect. Second person uses "you" to talk directly to the audience. However, there are no "you's" in the narrative, so Choice *B* is incorrect. Finally, all stories have *some kind* of person, so Choice *D* is incorrect.

38. B: She wanted to keep them away from harm. Choice *A* is incorrect; the passage mentions nothing about a science experiment. Choice *C* is incorrect; the passage does not mention Sylvia wanting to give the bees to her father. Finally, Choice *D* is incorrect; although Sylvia's mother *is* terrified of the bees, this isn't her motivation for putting them inside a jar.

39. A: This passage is chronologically ordered, which means it goes from a beginning to an end in a logical way. Cause and effect order is when a topic goes from talking about a specific cause to its effects, and this is incorrect. Problem to solution is more of a formal paper where the narrative depicts a problem and then offers a solution at the end, so Choice *C* is incorrect. Finally, sequential order is similar to chronological order, but it is more like step-by-step instructions, so Choice *D* is incorrect.

40. C: Freedom. If we had to choose one theme, it would probably be freedom. The theme is posed at the end of the passage, when Sylvia's mother basically asks her if she enjoys her own freedom playing outside. Sylvia realizes that she does and that the bees would probably enjoy that freedom as well, despite the dangers of being outdoors. The other answer choices are incorrect.

Verbal Section

Test takers encounter two parts in the verbal section of the Middle Level SSAT. In the first part, the vocabulary section, questions address the test taker's understanding of language and the meanings of different words. The second part is the analogy section, which assesses the test taker's ability to logically relate words to one another.

The vocabulary words are pulled from all areas of study and are of age-appropriate difficulty. Words may include those encountered specifically in science class, technology-related, social studies, mathematics, and language arts. Successful test takers should think about the parts of a word and the structure of the English language, including things like:

- Word origins
- Root words
- Prefixes
- Suffixes
- Words with multiple meanings

Synonyms

This portion of the exam is specifically constructed to test vocabulary skills and the ability to discern the best answer that matches the provided word. Unlike verbal analogies, which will test communication skills and problem-solving abilities along with vocabulary, these questions chiefly test vocabulary knowledge by asking test takers to select the best synonym for the provided word. While logic and reasoning come into play in this section, they are not as heavily emphasized as with the analogies. A prior knowledge of what the words mean is helpful in order to answer correctly. If the meaning of the words is unknown, that's fine, too. Strategies should be used to rule out false answers and choose the correct ones. Here are some study strategies for an optimum performance.

Format of the Questions

The synonyms questions are very simple in construction. Instead of a comparison of words with an underlying connection, like the verbal analogies, the prompt is just a single word. There are no special directions, alternate meanings, or analogies to work with. The objective is to analyze the given word and then choose the answer that means the same thing or is closest in meaning to the given word. Note the example below:

Blustery

    a. Hard
    b. Windy
    c. Mythical
    d. Stoney
    e. Corresponding

All of the questions on the Synonyms portion will appear exactly like the above sample. This is generally the standard layout throughout other exams, so some test-takers may already be familiar with the structure. The principle remains the same. At the top of the section, clear directions will be given to choose the answer that most precisely defines the given word. In this case, the answer is windy (B), since windy and blustery are synonymous.

Preparation

In truth, there is no set way to prepare for this portion of the exam that will guarantee a perfect score. This is simply because the words used on the test are unpredictable. There is no set list provided to study from. The definition of the provided word needs to be determined on the spot. This sounds challenging, but there are still ways to prepare mentally for the test. It may help to expand your vocabulary a little each day. Several resources are available, in books and online, that collect words and definitions that tend to show up frequently on standardized tests. Knowledge of words can increase the strength of your vocabulary.

Mindset is key. The meanings of challenging words can often be found by relying on the past experiences of the test-taker to help deduce the correct answer. How? Well, test-takers have been talking their entire lives—knowing words and how words work. It helps to have a positive mindset from the start. It's unlikely that all definitions of words will be known immediately, but the answer can still be found. There are aspects of words that are recognizable to help discern the correct answers and eliminate the incorrect ones. Here are some of the factors that contribute to word meanings!

Word Origins and Roots

Studying a foreign language in school, particularly Latin or any of the romance languages (Latin-influenced), is advantageous. English is a language highly influenced by Latin and Greek words. The roots of much of the English vocabulary have Latin origins; these roots can bind many words together and often allude to a shared definition. Here's an example:

Fervent

    a. Lame
    b. Joyful
    c. Thorough
    d. Boiling
    e. Cunning

Fervent descends from the Latin word, *fervere*, which means "to boil or glow" and figuratively means "impassioned." The Latin root present in the word is *ferv*, which is what gives fervent the definition: showing great warmth and spirit or spirited, hot, glowing. This provides a link to boiling (D) just by root word association, but there's more to analyze. Among the other choices, none relate to fervent. The word lame (A) means crippled, disabled, weak, or inadequate. None of these match with fervent. While being fervent can reflect joy, joyful (B) directly describes "a great state of happiness," while fervent is simply expressing the idea of having very strong feelings—not necessarily joy. Thorough (C) means complete, perfect, painstaking, or with mastery; while something can be done thoroughly and fervently, none of these words match fervent as closely as boiling does. Cunning (E) means crafty, deceiving or with ingenuity or dexterity. Doing something fervently does not necessarily mean it is done with dexterity. Not only does boiling connect in a linguistic way, but also in the way it is used in our language. While boiling can express being physically hot and undergoing a change, boiling is also used to reflect emotional states. People say they are "boiling over" when in heighted emotional states; "boiling mad" is another expression. Boiling, like fervent, also embodies a sense of heightened intensity. This makes boiling the best choice!

The Latin root *ferv* is seen in other words such as fervor, fervid, and even ferment. All of them are connected to and can be described by boil or glow, whether it is in a physical sense or in a metaphorical one. Such a pattern can be seen in other word sets! Here's another example:

Gracious

    a. Fruitful
    b. Angry
    c. Grateful
    d. Understood
    e. Overheard

This one's a little easier; the answer is grateful (C), because both words mean thankful! Even if the meanings of both words are known, there's a connection found by looking at the beginnings of both words: *gra/grat*. Once again, there is a root that stretches back to classical language. Both terms come from the Latin, *gratis*, which literally means "thanks."

Understanding root words can help identify the meaning in a lot of word choices, and help the test-taker grasp the nature of the given word. Many dictionaries, both in book form and online, offer information on the origins of words, which highlight these roots. When studying for the test, it helps to look up an unfamiliar word for its definition and then check to see if it has a root that can be connected to any of the other terms.

Pay Attention to Prefixes

The prefix of a word can actually reveal a lot about its definition. Many prefixes are actually Greco-Roman roots as well—but these are more familiar and a lot easier to recognize! When encountering any unfamiliar words, try looking at prefixes to discern the definition and then compare that with the choices. The prefix should be determined to help find the word's meaning. Here's an example question:

Premeditate

    a. Sporadic
    b. Calculated
    c. Interfere
    d. Determined
    e. Noble

With premeditate, there's the common prefix *pre*. This helps draw connections to other words like prepare or preassemble. *Pre* refers to "before, already being, or having already." Meditate means to think or plan. Premeditate means to think or plan beforehand with intent. Therefore, a term that deals with thinking or planning should be found, but also something done in preparation. Among the word choices, noble (E) and determined (D) are both adjectives with no hint of being related to something done before or in preparation. These choices are incorrect. Sporadic (A) refers to events happening in irregular patterns, so this is quite the opposite of premeditated. Interfere (C) also has nothing to do with premeditate; it goes counter to premeditate in a way similar to sporadic. Calculated (B), however, fits! A route and the cost of starting a plan can be calculated. Calculated refers to acting with a full awareness of consequences, so inherently planning is involved. In fact, calculated is synonymous with premeditated, thus making it the correct choice. Just by paying attention to a prefix, the doors to a meaning can open to help easily figure out which word would be the best choice. Here's another example.

Regain

  a. Erupt
  b. Ponder
  c. Seek
  d. Recoup
  e. Enamor

Recoup (D) is the right answer. The prefix *re* often appears in front of words to give them the meaning of occurring again. Regain means to repossess something that was lost. Recoup, which also has the *re* prefix, literally means to regain. In this example, both the given word and the answer share the *re* prefix, which makes the pair easy to connect. However, don't rely only on prefixes to choose an answer. Make sure to analyze all options before marking an answer. Going through the other words in this sample, none of them come close to meaning regain except recoup. After checking to make sure that recoup is the best matching word, then mark it!

Positive Versus Negative Sounding Words

Another tool for the mental toolbox is simply distinguishing whether a word has a positive or negative connotation. Like electrical wires, words carry energy; they are crafted to draw certain attention and to have certain strength to them. Words can be described as positive and uplifting (a stronger word) or they can be negative and scathing (a stronger word). Sometimes they are neutral—having no particular connotation. Distinguishing how a word is supposed to be interpreted will not only help learn its definition, but also draw parallels with word choices. While it's true that words must usually be taken in the context of how they are used, word definitions have inherent meanings as well. So, they have a distinct vibe to pick up on. Here is an example.

Excellent

  a. Fair
  b. Optimum
  c. Reasonable
  d. Negative
  e. Agitation

As you know, excellent is a very positive word. It refers to something being better than good, above average. In this sample, negative (D) and agitation (E) can easily be eliminated because these are both words with negative connotations. Reasonable (C) is more or less a neutral word: it's not bad but it doesn't communicate the higher quality that excellent represents. It's just, well, reasonable. This leaves the possible choices of fair (A) and optimum (B). Or does it? Fair *is* a positive word; it's used to describe things that are good, even beautiful. But in the modern context, fair is defined as good, but somewhat average or just decent: "You did a fairly good job." or, "That was fair." On the other hand, optimum is positive and is a stronger word. Optimum describes the most favorable outcome. This makes optimum the best word choice that matches excellent in both strength and connotation. Not only are the two words positive, but they also express the same level of positivity! Here's another example:

Repulse

    a. Draw
    b. Encumber
    c. Force
    d. Disgust
    e. Magnify

Repulse sounds negative when said. It is commonly used in the context of something being repulsive, disgusting, or that which is distasteful. It's also defined as an attack that drives people away. This tells us we need a word that also carries a negative meaning. Magnify (E) is positive, while draw (A) and force (C) are both neutral. Encumber (B) and disgust (D) are negative. Disgust is a stronger negative than encumber. Of all the words given, only disgust directly defines a feeling of distaste and aversion that is synonymous with repulse, and matches in both negativity and strength.

Parts of Speech

It is often very helpful to determine the part of speech of a word. Is it an adjective, adverb, noun, or verb, etc.? Often the correct answer will also be the same part of speech as the given word. Isolate the part of speech and what it describes and look for an answer choice that also describes the same part of speech. For example: if the given word is an adverb describing an action word, then look for another adverb describing an action word.

Swiftly

    a. Fast
    b. Quietly
    c. Angry
    d. Sudden
    e. Quickly

Swiftly is an adverb that describes the speed of an action. Angry (C), fast (A), and sudden (D) can be eliminated because they are not adverbs, and quietly (B) can be eliminated because it does not describe speed. This leaves quickly (E), which is the correct answer. Fast and sudden may throw off some test-takers because they both describe speed, but quickly matches more closely because it is an adverb, and swiftly is also an adverb.

Place the Word in a Sentence

Often it is easier to discern the meaning of a word if it is used in a sentence. If the given word can be used in a sentence, then try replacing it with some of the answer choices to see which words seem to make sense in the same sentence. Here's an example.

Remarkable

    a. Often
    b. Capable
    c. Outstanding
    d. Shining
    e. Excluding

A sentence can be formed with the word remarkable. "My grade point average is remarkable." None of the examples make sense when replacing the word remarkable in the sentence other than the word outstanding (C), so outstanding is the obvious answer. Shining (D) is also a word with a positive connotation, but outstanding fits better in the sentence.

Pick the Closest Answer

As the answer choices are reviewed, two scenarios might stand out. An exact definition match might not be found for the given word among the choices, or there are several word choices that can be considered synonymous to the given word. This is intentionally done to test the ability to draw parallels between the words to produce an answer that best fits the prompt word. Again, the closest fitting word will be the answer. Even when facing these two circumstances, finding the one word that fits best is the proper strategy. Here's an example:

Insubordination

    a. Cooperative
    b. Disciplined
    c. Rebel
    d. Contagious
    e. Wild

Insubordination refers to a defiance or utter refusal of authority. Looking over the choices, none of these terms provide definite matches to insubordination like insolence, mutiny, or misconduct would. This is fine; the answer doesn't have to be a perfect synonym. The choices don't reflect insubordination in any way, except rebel (C). After all, when rebel is used as a verb, it means to act against authority. It's also used as a noun: someone who goes against authority. Therefore, rebel is the best choice.

As with the verbal analogies section, being a detective is a good course to take. Two or even three choices might be encountered that could be the answer. However, the answer that most perfectly fits the prompt word's meaning is the best answer. Choices should be narrowed one word at a time. The least-connected word should be eliminated first and then proceed until one word is left that is the closest synonym.

Sequence

    a. List
    b. Range
    c. Series
    d. Replicate
    e. Iconic

A sequence reflects a particular order in which events or objects follow. The two closest options are list (A) and series (C). Both involve grouping things together, but which fits better? Consider each word more carefully. A list is comprised of items that fit in the same category, but that's really it. A list doesn't have to follow any particular order; it's just a list. On the other hand, a series is defined by events happening in a set order. A series relies on sequence, and a sequence can be described as a series. Thus, series is the correct answer!

For both portions of the Verbal Section in the Middle Level, SSAT, the following information about English language usage can provide helpful background knowledge to successfully answer questions. While some of this information has previously been touched upon, test takers can benefit from further explanation for several of these concepts.

Verbal Analogies

What are Verbal Analogies?

Analogies compare two different things that have a relationship or some similarity. For example, a basic analogy is apple is to fruit as cucumber is to vegetable. This analogy points out the category under which each item falls. On the SSAT, the final term (vegetable, in this case) will be blank and must be filled in from the multiple choices, selecting the word that best demonstrates the relationship in the first pair of words. Other analogies include words that are *synonyms*, which are words that share similar meanings to one another. For example, big and large are synonyms and tired and sleepy are also synonyms. Verbal analogy questions can be difficult because they require the test taker to demonstrate an understanding of small differences and similarities in both word meanings and word relationships.

Layout of the Questions

Verbal analogy sections are on other standardized tests such as the SAT. The format on the SSAT remains basically the same. First, two words are paired together that provide a frame for the analogy. Then, you are given a third word. You must find the relationship between the first two words, and then choose the fourth word to match the relationship to the third word. It may help to think of it like this: A is to B as C is to D. Examine the breakdown below:

Apple (A) is to fruit (B) as carrot (C) is to vegetable (D).

As shown above, there are four words: the first three are given and the fourth word is the answer that must be found. The first two words are given to set up the kind of analogy that is to be replicated for the next pair. We see that apple is paired with fruit. In the first pair, a specific food item, apple, is paired to the food group category it corresponds with, which is fruit. When presented with the third word in the verbal analogy, carrot, a word must be found that best matches carrot in the way that fruit matched with apple. Again, carrot is a specific food item, so a match should be found with the appropriate food group: vegetable! Here's a sample prompt:

Morbid is to dead as jovial is to

    a. Hate.
    b. Fear.
    c. Disgust.
    d. Happiness.
    e. Desperation.

As with the apple and carrot example, here is an analogy frame in the first two words: morbid and dead. Again, this will dictate how the next two words will correlate with one another. The definition of morbid is: described as or appealing to an abnormal and unhealthy interest in disturbing and unpleasant subjects, particularly death and disease. In other words, morbid can mean ghastly or death-like, which is why the word dead is paired with it. Dead relates to morbid because it describes morbid. With this in mind, jovial becomes the focus. Jovial means joyful, so out of all the choices given, the closest answer describing jovial is happiness (D).

Prompts on the exam will be structured just like the one above. "A is to B as C is to ?" will be given, where the answer completes the second pair. Or sometimes, "A is to B as ? is to ?" is given, where the second pair of words must be found that replicate the relationship between the first pair. The only things that will change are the words and the relationships between the words provided.

Discerning the Correct Answer

While it wouldn't hurt in test preparation to expand vocabulary, verbal analogies are all about delving into the words themselves and finding the right connection, the right word that will fit an analogy. People preparing for the test shouldn't think of themselves as human dictionaries, but rather as detectives. Remember that the first two words that are connected dictates the second pair. From there, picking the correct answer or simply eliminating the ones that aren't correct is the best strategy.

Just like a detective, a test-taker needs to carefully examine the first two words of the analogy for clues. It's good to get in the habit of asking the questions: What do the two words have in common? What makes them related or unrelated? How can a similar relationship be replicated with the word I'm given and the answer choices? Here's another example:

Pillage is to steal as meander is to

    a. Stroll.
    b. Burgle.
    c. Cascade.
    d. Accelerate.
    e. Pinnacle.

Why is pillage paired with steal? In this example, pillage and steal are synonymous: they both refer to the act of stealing. This means that the answer is a word that means the same as meander, which is stroll. In this case, the defining relationship in the whole analogy was a similar definition.

What if test-takers don't know what stroll or meander mean, though? Using logic helps to eliminate choices and pick the correct answer. Looking closer into the contexts of the words pillage and steal, here are a few facts: these are things that humans do; and while they are actions, these are not necessarily types of movement. Again, pick a word that will not only match the given word, but best completes the relationship. It wouldn't make sense that burgle (B) would be the correct choice because meander doesn't have anything to do with stealing, so that eliminates burgle. Pinnacle (E) also can be eliminated because this is not an action at all but a position or point of reference. Cascade (C) refers to pouring or falling, usually in the context of a waterfall and not in reference to people, which means we can eliminate cascade as well. While people do accelerate when they move, they usually do so under additional circumstances: they accelerate while running or driving a car. All three of the words we see in the analogy are actions that can be done independently of other factors. Therefore, accelerate (D) can be eliminated, and stroll (A) should be chosen. Stroll and meander both refer to walking or wandering, so this fits perfectly.

The *process of elimination* will help rule out wrong answers. However, the best way to find the correct answer is simply to differentiate the correct answer from the other choices. For this, test-takers should go back to asking questions, starting with the chief question: What's the connection? There are actually many ways that connections can be found between words. The trick is to look for the answer that is consistent with the relationship between the words given. What is the prevailing connection? Here are a few different ways verbal analogies can be formed.

Finding Connections in Word Analogies

Categories

One of the easiest ways to choose the correct answer in word analogies is simply to group the words. Ask if the words can be compartmentalized into *distinct categories*. Here are some examples:

Terrier is to dog as mystery is to

    a. Thriller.
    b. Murder.
    c. Detective.
    d. Novel.
    e. Investigation.

This one might have been a little confusing, but when looking at the first two words in the analogy, this is clearly one in which a category is the prevailing theme. Think about it: a terrier is a type of dog. While there are several breeds of dogs that can be categorized as a terrier, in the end, all terriers are still dogs. Therefore, mystery needs to be grouped into a category. Murders, detectives, and investigations can all be involved in a mystery plot, but a murder (B), a detective (C), or an investigation (E) is not necessarily a mystery. A thriller (A) is a purely fictional concept, a kind of story or film, just like a mystery. A thriller can describe a mystery, but the same issue appears as the other choices. What about novel (D)? For one thing, it's distinct from all the other terms. A novel isn't a component of a mystery, but a mystery can be a type of novel. The relationship fits: a terrier is a type of dog, just like a mystery is a type of novel.

Synonym/Antonym

Some analogies are based on words meaning the same thing or expressing the same idea. Sometimes it's the complete opposite!

Marauder is to brigand as

    a. King is to peasant.
    b. Juice is to orange.
    c. Soldier is to warrior.
    d. Engine is to engineer.
    e. Paper is to photocopier.

Here, soldier is to warrior (C) is the correct answer. Marauders and brigands are both thieves. They are synonyms. The only pair of words that fits this analogy is soldier and warrior because both terms describe combatants who fight.

Cap is to shoe as jacket is to

    a. Ring.
    b. T-shirt.
    c. Vest.
    d. Glasses.
    e. Pants.

Opposites are at play here because a cap is worn on the head/top of the person, while a shoe is worn on the foot/bottom. A jacket is worn on top of the body too, so the opposite of jacket would be pants (E) because these are worn on the bottom. Often the prompts on the test provide a synonym or antonym relationship. Just consider if the sets in the prompt reflect similarity or stark difference.

Parts of a Whole

Another thing to consider when first looking at an analogy prompt is whether the words presented come together in some way. Do they express parts of the same item? Does one word complete the other? Are they connected by process or function?

Tire is to car as

    a. Wing is to bird.
    b. Oar is to boat.
    c. Box is to shelf.
    d. Hat is to head.
    e. Knife is to sheath.

We know that the tire fits onto the car's wheels and this is what enables the car to drive on roads. The tire is part of the car. This is the same relationship as oar is to boat (B). The oars are attached onto a boat and enable a person to move and navigate the boat on water. At first glance, wing is to bird (A) seems to fit too, since a wing is a part of a bird that enables it to move through the air. However, since a tire and car are not alive and transport people, oar and boat fit better because they are also not alive and they transport people. Subtle differences between answer choices should be found.

Other Relationships

There are a number of other relationships to look for when solving verbal analogies. Some relationships focus on one word being a *characteristic/NOT a characteristic* of the other word. Sometimes the first word is the *source/comprised of* the second word. Still, other words are related by their *location*. Some analogies have *sequential* relationships, and some are *cause/effect* relationships. There are analogies that show *creator/provider* relationships with the *creation/provision*. Another relationship might compare an *object* with its *function* or a *user* with his or her *tool*. An analogy may focus on a *change of grammar* or a *translation of language*. Finally, one word of an analogy may have a relationship to the other word in its *intensity*.

The type of relationship between the first two words of the analogy should be determined before continuing to analyze the second set of words. One effective method of determining a relationship between two words is to form a comprehensible sentence using both words. Then plug the answer choices into the same sentence. For example in the analogy: *Bicycle is to handlebars as car is to steering wheel*, a sentence could be formed that says: A bicycle navigates using its handlebars; therefore, a car navigates using its steering wheel. If the second sentence makes sense, then the correct relationship likely is found. A sentence may be more complex depending on the relationship between the first two words in the analogy. An example of this may be: *food is to dishwasher as dirt is to carwash.* The formed sentence may be: A dishwasher cleans food off of dishes in the same way that a carwash cleans dirt off of a car.

Dealing with Multiple Connections

There are many other ways to draw connections between word sets. Several word choices might form an analogy that would fit the word set in your prompt. This is when an analogy from multiple angles needs to be explored. Several words might even fit in a relationship. If so, which one is an even closer match than the others? The framing word pair is another important point to consider. Can one or both words be interpreted as actions or ideas, or are they purely objects? Here's a question where words could have alternate meanings:

Hammer is to nail as saw is to

    a. Electric.
    b. Hack.
    c. Cut.
    d. Machete.
    e. Groove.

Looking at the question above, it becomes clear that the topic of the analogy involves construction tools. Hammers and nails are used in concert, since the hammer is used to pound the nail. The logical first thing to do is to look for an object that a saw would be used on. Seeing that there is no such object among the answer choices, a test-taker might begin to worry. After all, that seems to be the choice that would complete the analogy—but that doesn't mean it's the only choice that may fit. Encountering questions like this tests the ability to see multiple connections between words. Don't get stuck thinking that words have to be connected in a single way. The first two words given can be verbs instead of just objects. To hammer means to hit or beat; oftentimes it refers to beating something into place. This is also what nail means when it is used as a verb. Here are the word choices that reveal the answer.

First, it's known that a saw, well, saws. It uses a steady motion to cut an object, and indeed to saw means to cut! Cut (C) is one of our answer choices, but the other options should be reviewed. While some tools are electric (a), the use of power in the tools listed in the analogy isn't a factor. Again, it's been established that these word choices are not tools in this context. Therefore, machete (D) is also ruled out because machete is also not a verb. Another important thing to consider is that while a machete is a tool that accomplishes a similar purpose as a saw, the machete is used in a slicing motion rather than a sawing/cutting motion. The verb that describes machete is hack (B), another choice that can be ruled out. A machete is used to hack at foliage. However, a saw does not hack. Groove (E) is just a term that has nothing to do with the other words, so this choice can be eliminated easily. This leaves cut (C), which confirms that this is the word needed to complete the analogy!

Vocabulary

Parts of Speech

Also referred to as word classes, parts of speech refer to the various categories in which words are placed. Words can be placed in any one or a combination of the following categories:

- Nouns
- Determiners
- Pronouns
- Verbs
- Adjectives
- Adverbs
- Prepositions
- Conjunctions

Understanding the various parts of speech used in the English language helps readers to better understand the written language.

Nouns

Nouns are defined as any word that represents a person, place, animal, object, or idea. Nouns can identify a person's title or name, a person's gender, and a person's nationality, such as banker, commander-in-chief, female, male, or an American.

With animals, nouns identify the kingdom, phylum, class, etc. For example: animal is elephant; phylum is chordata; or class is mammalia.

When identifying places, nouns refer to a physical location, a general vicinity, or the proper name of a city, state, or country. Some examples include the desert, the East, Phoenix, Arizona, or the United States.

There are eight types of nouns: common, proper, countable, uncountable, concrete, abstract, compound, and collective.

Common nouns are used in general terms, without specific identification. Examples include girl, boy, country, or school. Proper nouns refer to the proper name given to people, places, animals, or entities, such as Melissa, Martin, Italy, or Harvard.

Countable nouns can be counted: one car, two cars, or three cars. Uncountable nouns cannot be counted, such as air, liquid, or gas.

To be abstract is to exist, but only in thought or as an idea. An abstract noun cannot be physically touched, seen, smelled, heard, or tasted. These include chivalry, day, fear, thought, truth, friendship, or freedom.

To be concrete is to be seen, touched, tasted, heard, and/or smelled. Examples include pie, snow, tree, bird, desk, hair, or dog.

A compound noun is another term for an open compound word. Any noun that is written as two nouns that together form a specific meaning is a compound noun, such as post office, ice cream, or swimming pool.

A collective noun is formed by grouping three or more words to create one meaning. Examples include bunch of flowers, herd of elephants, flock of birds, or school of fish.

Determiners

Determiners modify a noun and usually refer to something specific. Determiners fall into one of four categories: articles, demonstratives, quantifiers, or possessive determiners.

Articles can be both definite articles, as in *the*, and indefinite as in *a, an, some,* or *any*:

> *The* man with *the* red hat.

> *A* flower growing in *the* yard.

> *Any* person who visits *the* store.

There are four different types of demonstratives: this, that, these, and those.

True demonstrative words will not directly precede the noun of the sentence, but will *be* the noun. Some examples:

> *This* is the one.

> *That* is the place.

> *Those* are the files.

Once a demonstrative is placed directly in front of the noun, it becomes a demonstrative pronoun:

> *This* one is perfect.

> *That* place is lovely.

> *Those* boys are annoying.

Quantifiers proceed nouns to give additional information for how much or how many. They can be used with countable and uncountable nouns:

> She bought *plenty* of apples.

> *Few* visitors came.

> I got a *little* change.

Possessive determiners, sometimes called possessive adjectives, indicate possession. They are the possessive forms of personal pronouns, such as for my, your, hers, his, its, their, or our:

> That is *my* car.

> Tom rode *his* bike today.

> Those papers are *hers*.

Pronouns
Pronouns are words that stand in place of nouns. There are three different types of pronouns: subjective pronouns (I, you, he, she, it, we, they), objective pronouns (me, you, him, her it, us, them), and possessive pronouns (mine, yours, his, hers, ours, theirs).

You'll see some words are found in more than one pronoun category. See examples and clarifications below:

> *You* are going to the movies.

You is a subjective pronoun; it is the subject of the sentence and is performing the action.

> I threw the ball to *you*.

You is an objective pronoun; it is receiving the action and is the object of the sentence.

> We saw *her* at the movies.

Her is an objective pronoun; it is receiving the action and is the object of the sentence.

The house across the street from the park is *hers.*

Hers is a possessive pronoun; it shows possession of the house and is used as a possessive pronoun.

Verbs
Verbs are words in a sentence that show action or state. Just as there can be no sentence without a subject, there can be no sentence without a verb. In these sentences, notice verbs in the present, past, and future tenses. To form some tenses in the future and in the past requires auxiliary, or helping, verbs:

I *see* the neighbors across the street.

See is an action.

We *were eating* at the picnic.

Eating is the main action, and the verb *were* is the past tense of the verb *to be,* and is the helping or auxiliary verb that places the sentence in the past tense.

You *will turn* 20 years of age next month.

Turn is the main verb, but to show a future tense, *will* is the helping verb to show future tense of the verb *to be.*

Adjectives
Adjectives are a special group of words used to modify or describe a noun. Adjectives provide more information about the noun they modify. For example:

The boy went to school. (There is no adjective.)

Rewrite the sentence, adding an adjective to further describe the boy and/or the school:

The *young* boy went to the *old* school. (The adjective *young* describes the boy, and the adjective *old* describes the school.)

Adverbs
Adverb can play one of two roles: to modify the adjective or to modify the verb. For example:

The young boy went to the old school.

We can further describe the adjectives *young* and *old* with adverbs placed directly in front of the adjectives:

The *very* young boy went to the *very* old school. (The adverb *very* further describes the adjectives *young* and *old*.)

Other examples of using adverbs to further describe verbs:

The boy *slowly* went to school.

The boy *quickly* went to school.

The adverbs *slowly* and *quickly* further modify the verbs.

<u>Prepositions</u>

Prepositions are special words that generally precede a noun. Prepositions clarify the relationship between the subject and another word or element in the sentence. They clarify time, place, and the positioning of subjects and objects in a sentence. Common prepositions in the English language include: near, far, under, over, on, in, between, beside, of, at, until, behind, across, after, before, for, from, to, by, and with.

<u>Conjunctions</u>

Conjunctions are a group of unique words that connect clauses or sentences. They also work to coordinate words in the same clause. It is important to choose an appropriate conjunction based on the meaning of the sentence. Consider these sentences:

> I really like the flowers, *however* the smell is atrocious.

> I really like the flowers, *besides* the smell is atrocious.

The conjunctions *however* and *besides* act as conjunctions, connecting the two ideas: *I really like the flowers,* and, *the smell is atrocious*. In the second sentence, the conjunction *besides* makes no sense and would confuse the reader. You must consider the message you wish to convey and choose conjunctions that clearly state that message without ambiguity.

Some conjunctions introduce an opposing opinion, thought, or fact. They can also reinforce an opinion, introduce an explanation, reinforce cause and effect, or indicate time. For example:

> She wishes to go to the movies, *but* she doesn't have the money. (Opposition)

> The professor became ill, *so* the class was postponed. (Cause and effect)

> They visited Europe *before* winter came. (Time)

Each conjunction serves a specific purpose in uniting two separate ideas. Below are common conjunctions in the English language:

Opposition	Cause & Effect	Reinforcement	Time	Explanation
however	therefore	besides	afterward	for example
nevertheless	as a result	anyway	before	in other words
but	because of this	after all	firstly	for instance
although	consequently	furthermore	next	such as

Synonym Practice Questions

1. DEDUCE
   a. Explain
   b. Win
   c. Reason
   d. Gamble
   e. Undo

2. ELUCIDATE
   a. Learn
   b. Enlighten
   c. Plan
   d. Corroborate
   e. Conscious

3. VERIFY
   a. Criticize
   b. Change
   c. Teach
   d. Substantiate
   e. Resolve

4. INSPIRE
   a. Motivate
   b. Impale
   c. Exercise
   d. Patronize
   e. Collaborate

5. PERCEIVE
   a. Sustain
   b. Collect
   c. Prove
   d. Lead
   e. Comprehend

6. NOMAD
   a. Munching
   b. Propose
   c. Wanderer
   d. Conscientious
   e. Blissful

7. PERPLEXED
   a. Annoyed
   b. Vengeful
   c. Injured
   d. Confused
   e. Prepared

8. LYRICAL
   a. Whimsical
   b. Vague
   c. Fruitful
   d. Expressive
   e. Playful

9. BREVITY
   a. Dullness
   b. Dangerous
   c. Brief
   d. Ancient
   e. Calamity

10. IRATE
    a. Anger
    b. Knowledge
    c. Tired
    d. Confused
    e. Taciturn

11. LUXURIOUS
    a. Faded
    b. Bright
    c. Lavish
    d. Inconsiderate
    e. Overwhelming

12. IMMOBILE
    a. Fast
    b. Slow
    c. Eloquent
    d. Vivacious
    e. Sedentary

13. OVERBEARING
    a. Neglect
    b. Overactive
    c. Clandestine
    d. Formidable
    e. Amicable

14. PREVENT
    a. Avert
    b. Rejoice
    c. Endow
    d. Fulfill
    e. Ensure

15. REPLENISH
    a. Falsify
    b. Hindsight
    c. Dwell
    d. Refresh
    e. Nominate

16. REGALE
    a. Remember
    b. Grow
    c. Outnumber
    d. Entertain
    e. Bore

17. WEARY
    a. tired
    b. clothing
    c. happy
    d. hot
    e. whiny

18. VAST
    a. Rapid
    b. Expansive
    c. Small
    d. Ocean
    e. Uniform

19. DEMONSTRATE
    a. Tell
    b. Show
    c. Build
    d. Complete
    e. Make

20. ORCHARD
    a. Flower
    b. Fruit
    c. Grove
    d. Peach
    e. Farm

21. TEXTILE
    a. Fabric
    b. Document
    c. Mural
    d. Ornament
    e. Knit

22. OFFSPRING
    a. Bounce
    b. Parent
    c. Music
    d. Child
    e. Skip

23. PERMIT
    a. Law
    b. Parking
    c. Crab
    d. Jail
    e. Allow

24. WOMAN
    a. Man
    b. Lady
    c. Women
    d. Girl
    e. Mother

25. ROTATION
    a. Wheel
    b. Year
    c. Spin
    d. Flip
    e. Orbit

26. CONSISTENT
    a. Stubborn
    b. Contains
    c. Sticky
    d. Texture
    e. Steady

27. PRINCIPLE
    a. Principal
    b. Leader
    c. President
    d. Foundation
    e. Royal

28. PERIMETER
   a. Outline
   b. Area
   c. Side
   d. Volume
   e. Inside

29. SYMBOL
   a. Drum
   b. Music
   c. Clang
   d. Emblem
   e. Text

30. GERMINATE
   a. Doctor
   b. Sick
   c. Infect
   d. Plants
   e. Grow

Verbal Analogies Practice Questions

1. *Cat* is to *paws* as
    a. Giraffe is to neck.
    b. Elephant is to ears.
    c. Horse is to hooves.
    d. Snake is to skin.
    e. Turtle is to shell.

2. *Dancing* is to *rhythm* as *singing* is to
    a. Pitch.
    b. Mouth.
    c. Sound.
    d. Volume.
    e. Words.

3. *Towel* is to *dry* as *hat* is to
    a. Cold.
    b. Warm.
    c. Expose.
    d. Cover.
    e. Top.

4. *Sand* is to *glass* as
    a. Protons are to atoms.
    b. Ice is to snow.
    c. Seeds are to plants.
    d. Water is to steam.
    e. Air is to wind.

5. *Design* is to *create* as *allocate* is to
    a. Finish.
    b. Manage.
    c. Multiply.
    d. Find.
    e. Distribute.

6. *Books* are to *reading* as
    a. Movies are to making.
    b. Shows are to watching.
    c. Poetry is to writing.
    d. Scenes are to performing.
    e. Concerts are to music.

7. *Cool* is to *frigid* as *warm* is to
    a. Toasty.
    b. Summer.
    c. Sweltering.
    d. Hot.
    e. Mild.

8. *Buses* are to *rectangular prisms* as *globes* are to
    a. Circles.
    b. Maps.
    c. Wheels.
    d. Spheres.
    e. Movement.

9. *Backpacks* are to *textbooks* as
    a. Houses are to people.
    b. Fences are to trees.
    c. Plates are to food.
    d. Chalkboards are to chalk.
    e. Computers are to mice.

10. *Storm* is to *rainbow* as *sunset* is to
    a. Clouds.
    b. Sunrise.
    c. Breakfast.
    d. Bedtime.
    e. Stars.

11. *Falcon* is to *mice* as *giraffe* is to
    a. Leaves.
    b. Rocks.
    c. Antelope.
    d. Grasslands.
    e. Hamsters.

12. *Car* is to *motorcycle* as *speedboat* is to
    a. Raft.
    b. Jet-ski.
    c. Sailboat.
    d. Plane.
    e. Canoe.

13. *Arid* is to *damp* as *anxious* is to
    a. Happy.
    b. Petrified.
    c. Ireful.
    d. Confident.
    e. Sorrowful.

14. *Mechanic* is to *repair* as
    a. Mongoose is to cobra.
    b. Rider is to bicycle.
    c. Tree is to grow.
    d. Food is to eaten.
    e. Doctor is to heal.

15. *Whistle* is to *blow horn* as *painting* is to
    a. View.
    b. Criticize.
    c. Sculpture.
    d. Painter.
    e. Paintbrush.

16. *Paddle* is to *boat* as *keys* are to
    a. Unlock.
    b. Success.
    c. Illuminate.
    d. Piano.
    e. Keychain.

17. *Mountain* is to *peak* as *wave* is to
    a. Ocean.
    b. Surf.
    c. Fountain.
    d. Wavelength.
    e. Crest.

18. *Fluent* is to *communication* as
    a. Crater is to catastrophe.
    b. Gourmet is to cooking.
    c. Ink is to pen.
    d. Crow is to raven.
    e. Whistle is to whistler.

19. *Validate* is to *truth* as *conquer* is to
    a. Withdraw.
    b. Subjugate.
    c. Expand.
    d. Surrender.
    e. Expose.

20. *Winter* is to *autumn* as *summer* is to
    a. Vacation.
    b. Fall.
    c. Spring.
    d. March.
    e. Weather.

21. *Fiberglass* is to *surfboard* as
    a. Bamboo is to panda.
    b. Capital is to D.C.
    c. Copper is to penny.
    d. Flint is to mapping.
    e. Wind is to windmill.

22. *Myth* is to *explain* as *joke* is to
    a. Enlighten.
    b. Inspire.
    c. Collect.
    d. Laughter.
    e. Amuse.

23. *Cow* is to *milk* as:
    a. Horse is to cow
    b. Egg is to chicken
    c. Chicken is to egg
    d. Glass is to milk
    e. Milk is to glass

24. *Web* is to *spider* as *den* is to:
    a. Living room
    b. Eagle
    c. Fox
    d. Dog
    e. Turtle

25. *Sad* is to *blue* as *happy* is to:
    a. Glad
    b. Yellow
    c. Smiling
    d. Laugh
    e. Calm

26. *Door* is to *store* as *deal* is to:
    a. Money
    b. Purchase
    c. Sell
    d. Wheel
    d. Market

27. *Dog* is to *veterinarian* as *baby* is to
    a. Daycare
    b. Mother
    c. Puppy
    d. Babysitter
    e. Pediatrician

28. *Clock* is to *time* as:
    a. Ruler is to length
    b. Jet is to speed
    c. Alarm is to sleep
    d. Drum is to beat
    e. Watch is to wrist

29. *Wire* is to *electricity* as:
    a. Power is to lamp
    b. Pipe is to water
    c. Fire is to heat
    d. Heat is to fire
    e. Water is to pipe

30. *President* is to *Executive Branch* as _____ is to *Judicial Branch*.
    a. Supreme Court Justice
    b. Judge
    c. Senator
    d. Lawyer
    e. Congressmen

Synonym Answer Explanations

1. C: To deduce something is to figure it out using reasoning. Although this might cause a win and prompt an explanation to further understanding, the art of deduction is logical reasoning.

2. B: To elucidate, a light is figuratively shined on a previously unknown or confusing subject. This Latin root, "lux" meaning "light," prominently figures into the solution. Enlighten means to educate, or bring into the light.

3. D: Looking at the Latin word "veritas," meaning "truth," will yield a clue as to the meaning of verify. To verify is the act of finding or assessing the truthfulness of something. This usually means amassing evidence to substantiate a claim. Substantiate, of course, means to provide evidence to prove a point.

4. A: If someone is inspired, they are motivated to do something. Someone who is an inspiration motivates others to follow his or her example.

5. E: All the connotations of perceive involve the concept of seeing. Whether figuratively or literally, perceiving implies the act of understanding what is presented. Comprehending is synonymous with this understanding.

6. C: Nomadic tribes are those who, throughout history and even today, prefer to wander their lands instead of settling in any specific place. Wanderer best describes these people.

7. D: Perplexed means baffled or puzzled, which are synonymous with confused.

8. D: Lyrical is used to refer to something being poetic or song-like, characterized by showing enormous imagination and description. While the context of lyrical can be playful or even whimsical, the best choice is expressive, since whatever emotion lyrical may be used to convey in context will be expressive in nature.

9. C: Brevity literally means brief or concise. Note the similar beginnings of brevity and brief—from the Latin "brevis," meaning brief.

10. A: Irate means being in a state of anger. Clearly this is a negative word that can be paired with another word in kind. The closest word to match this is obviously anger. Research would also reveal that irate comes from the Latin "ira," which means anger.

11. C: Lavish is a synonym for luxurious—both describe elaborate and/or elegant lifestyles and/or settings.

12. E: Immobile obviously means "not able to move." The two best selections are B and E—but slow still implies some form of motion, whereas sedentary has the connotation of being seated and/or inactive for a significant portion of time and/or as a natural tendency.

13. B: Overbearing refers to domineering or being oppressive. This is emphasized in the "over" prefix, which emphasizes an excess in definitions. This prefix is also seen in overactive. Similar to overbearing, overacting reflects an excess of action.

14. A: The "pre" prefix describes something that occurs before an event. Prevent means to stop something before it happens. This leads to a word that relates to something occurring beforehand and, in a way, is preventive—wanting to stop something. Avert literally means to turn away or ward off an impending circumstance, making it the best fit.

15. D: Refresh is synonymous with replenish. Both words mean to restore or refill. Additionally, these terms do share the "re" prefix as well.

16. D: Regale literally means to amuse someone with a story. This is a very positive word; the best way to eliminate choices is to look for a term that matches regale in both positive context/sound and definition. Entertain is both a positive word and a synonym of regale.

17. A: Weary most closely means tired. Someone who is weary and tired may be whiny, but they do not necessarily mean the same thing.

18. B: Something that is vast is far-reaching and expansive. Choice D, ocean, may be described as vast but the word alone doesn't mean vast. The heavens or skies may also be described as vast. Someone's imagination or vocabulary can also be vast.

19. B: To demonstrate something means to show it. The word demonstration comes from demonstrate and a demonstration is a modeling or show-and-tell type of example that is usually visual.

20. C: An orchard is most like a grove because both are areas like plantations that grow different kinds of fruit. Peach is a type of fruit that may be grown in an orchard but it is not a synonym for orchard. Many citrus fruits are grown in groves but either word can be used to describe many fruit-bearing trees in one area. Choice *E*, farm, may have an orchard or grove on the property, but they are not the same thing and many farms do not grow fruit trees.

21. A: A textile is another word for a fabric. The most confusing alternative choice in this case is knit, because some textiles are knit but *textile* and *knit* are not synonyms and plenty of textiles are not knit.

22. D: Offspring are the children of parents. This word is especially common when talking about the animal kingdom, although it can be used with humans as well. *Offspring* does have the word *spring* in it, although it has nothing to do with bouncing or jumping. The other answer choice, parent, may be somewhat tricky because parents have offspring, but for this reason, they are not synonyms.

23. E: Permit can be a verb or a noun. As a verb, it means to allow or give authorization for something. As a noun, it generally refers to a document or something that has been authorized like a parking permit or driving permit, allowing the authorized individual to park or drive under the rules of the document.

24. B: A woman is a lady. Test takers must read carefully and remember the difference between *woman* and *women*. *Woman* refers to an individual lady or one person who is female, while *women* is the plural form and refers to more than one, or a group, of ladies. A woman may be a mother but not necessarily, and these words are not synonyms. A girl is a child and not yet a woman.

25. C: Rotation means to spin or turn, such as a wheel rotating on a car, although wheel does not *mean* rotation.

26. E: Something that is consistent is steady, predictable, reliable, or constant. The tricky one here is that the word *consistency* comes from the word consistent, and may describe a text or something that is sticky. *Consistent* also comes from the word *consist,* which means to contain (Choice *B*). Test takers must be discerning readers and knowledgeable about vocabulary to recognize the difference in these words and look for the true synonym of *consistent.*

27. D: A principle is a foundation or a guiding idea or belief. Someone with good moral character is described as having strong principles. Test takers must be careful not to get confused with the homonyms *principle* and *principal*, because these words have very different meanings. A principal is the leader of a school and the word principal also refers to the main or most important idea or thing.

28. A: Perimeter refers to the outline or borders of an object. Test takers may recognize that word from math class, where perimeter refers to the edges or distance around an enclosed shape. Some of the other answer choices refer to other math vocabulary encountered in geometry lessons, but do not have the same meaning as *perimeter.*

29. D: A symbol is an object, picture, or sign that is used to represent something. For example, a pink ribbon is a symbol for breast-cancer awareness and a flag can be a symbol for a country. The tricky part of this question was also knowing the meaning of *emblem,* which typically describes a design that represents a group or concept, much like a symbol. Emblems often appear on flags or a coat of arms.

30. E: Germinate means to develop or grow and most often refers to sprouting seeds as a new plant first breaks through the seed coat. It can also refer to the development of an idea. Choice *D* may be an attractive choice since plants germinate but germinate does not mean *plant.*

Verbal Analogies Practice Answers

1. C: This is a part/whole analogy. The common thread is what animals walk on. *A, B*, and *E* all describe signature parts of animals, but paws are not the defining feature of cats. While snakes travel on their skins, they do not walk.

2. A: This is a characteristic analogy. The connection lies in what observers will judge a performance on. While the other choices are also important, an off-key singer is as unpleasant as a dancer with no rhythm.

3. D: This is a use/tool analogy. The analogy focuses on an item's use. While hats are worn when it's cold with the goal of making the top of your head warm, this is not always guaranteed—their primary use is to provide cover. There is also the fact that not all hats are used to keep warm, but all hats cover the head.

4. D: This is a source/comprised of analogy. The common thread is addition of fire. Protons contribute to atoms and seeds grow into plants, but these are simple matters of building and growing without necessarily involving fire. Choices *B* and *E* relate objects that already have similar properties.

5. E: This is a synonym analogy. The determining factor is synonymous definition. Design and create are synonyms, as are allocate and distribute. Typically, items are found and allocated as part of management to finish a project, but these qualities are not innate in the word. Allocation generally refers to the division of commodities instead of multiplication.

6. B: This is a tool/use analogy. The common thread is audience response to an art form. *A, C*, and *D* deal with the creation of artwork instead of its consumption. Choice *E* describes a form of art instead of the audience engagement with such.

7. C: This is an intensity analogy. The common thread is degree of severity. While *A, D*, and *E* can all describe warmth, they don't convey the harshness of sweltering. Choice *B* simply describes a time when people may be more likely to think of warmth.

8. D: This is a characteristic analogy and is based on matching objects to their geometric shapes. Choice *A* is not correct because globes are three-dimensional, whereas circles exist in two dimensions. While wheels are three-dimensional, they are not always solid or perfectly round.

9. A: This is a tool/use analogy. The key detail of this analogy is the idea of enclosing or sealing items/people. When plates are filled with food, there is no way to enclose the item. While trees can be inside a fence, they can also be specifically outside of one.

10. E: This is a sequence of events analogy. The common thread is celestial cause-and-effect. Not everyone has breakfast or goes to bed after sunset. Sunrise is not typically thought of as the next interesting celestial event after sunsets. While clouds can develop after sunsets, they are also present before and during this activity. Stars, however, can be seen after dark.

11. A: This is a provider/provision analogy. The theme of this analogy is pairing a specific animal to their food source. Falcons prey on mice. Giraffes are herbivores and only eat one of the choices: leaves. Grasslands describe a type of landscape, not a food source for animals.

12. B: This is a category analogy. The common thread is motorized vehicles. While *A, C,* and *E* also describe vehicles that move on water, they are not motorized. Although relying on engines, planes are not a form of water transportation.

13. D: This is an antonym analogy. The prevailing connection is opposite meanings. While happy can be an opposite of anxious, it's also possible for someone to experience both emotions at once. Choices *B, C,* and *E* are also concurrent with anxious, not opposite.

14. E: This is a provider/provision analogy. This analogy looks at professionals and what their job is. Just as a mechanic's job is to repair machinery, a doctor works to heal patients.

15. C: This is a category analogy. Both whistles and blow horns are devices used to project/produce sound. Therefore, the analogy is based on finding something of a categorical nature. While Choices *A, B, D,* and *E* involve or describe painting, they do not pertain to a distinct discipline alongside painting. Sculpture, however, is another form of art and expression, just like painting.

16. D: This is a part/whole analogy. This analogy examines the relationship between two objects. Specifically, this analogy examines how one object connects to another object, with the first object(s) being the means by which people use the corresponding object to produce a result directly. People use a paddle to steer a boat, just as pressing keys on a piano produces music. Choices *B* and *C* can be metaphorically linked to keys but are unrelated. Choice *A* is related to keys but is a verb, not another object. Choice *E* is the trickiest alternative, but what's important to remember is that while keys are connected to key chains, there is no result just by having the key on a key chain.

17. E: This is a part/whole analogy. This analogy focuses on natural formations and their highest points. The peak of a mountain is its highest point just as the crest is the highest rise in a wave.

18. B: This is an intensity analogy. Fluent refers to how well one can communicate, while gourmet describes a standard of cooking. The analogy draws on degrees of a concept.

19. B: This is a synonym analogy, which relies on matching terms that are most closely connected. Validate refers to finding truth. Therefore, finding the term that best fits conquer is a good strategy. While nations have conquered others to expand their territory, they are ultimately subjugating those lands and people to their will. Therefore, subjugate is the best-fitting answer.

20. C: This is a sequence of events analogy. This analogy pairs one season with the season that precedes it. Winter is paired with autumn because autumn actually comes before winter. Out of all the answers only Choices *B* and *C* are actual seasons. Fall is another name for autumn, which comes after summer, not before. Spring, of course, is the season that comes before summer, making it the correct answer.

21. C: This is a source/comprised of analogy. This analogy focuses on pairing a raw material with an object that it's used to create. Fiberglass is used to build surfboards just as copper is used in the creation of pennies. While wind powers a windmill, there is no physical object produced, like with the fiberglass/surfboards pair.

22. E: This is an object/function analogy. The common thread between these words is that one word describes a kind of story and it is paired with the purpose of the story. Myth is/was told in order to explain fundamental beliefs and natural phenomena. While laughter can result from a joke, the purpose of telling a joke is to amuse the audience, thus making Choice *E* the right choice.

23. C: Cows produce milk so the question is looking for another pair that has a producer and their product. Horses don't produce cows (Choice A), glasses don't produce milk (Choice D) and milk doesn't produce a glass (Choice E). The correct choice is C: chicken is to egg. The tricky one here is Choice B, egg is to chicken, because it has the correct words but the wrong order, and therefore it reverses the relationship. Eggs don't produce chickens, so it doesn't work with the first part of the analogy: cow is to milk.

24. C: The first part of the analogy—web is to spider—describes the home (web) and who lives in it (spider), so the question is looking for what animal lives in a den. The best choice is C, fox. Living room is another word or a synonym for a den.

25. A: Sad and blue are synonyms because they are both describing the same type of mood. The word *blue* in this case is not referring to the color; therefore, although yellow is sometimes considered a "happy" color, the question isn't referring to blue as a color (or any color for that matter) and yellow and happy are not synonyms. Someone who is happy may laugh or smile, but these words are not synonyms for happy. Lastly, someone who is happy may be calm, although he or she could also be excited, and calm and happy are not synonyms. The best choice is glad.

26. D: The key to answering this question correctly is to recognize that the relationship between door and store are that the words rhyme. One may at first consider the fact that stores have doors, but after reviewing the other word choices and the given word *deal*, he or she should notice that none of the other words have this relationship. Instead, the answer choice should be one that rhymes with *deal*. Wheel and deal, although spelled differently, are rhyming words, and therefore the correct answer is *D*.

27. E: This question relies on the test takers knowledge of occupations. Dogs are taken care of by veterinarians so the solution is looking for who takes care of babies. However, this level of detail is not yet specific enough because mothers and babysitters can also take care of babies. Veterinarians take care of sick dogs and act as a medical doctor for pets. Therefore, with this higher level of specificity and detail, test takers should select pediatrician, because pediatricians are doctors for babies and children.

28. A: The relationship in the first half of the analogy is that clocks are used to measure time, so the second half of the analogy should have a tool that is used to measure something followed by what it measures. Rulers can be used to measure length, so that is the best choice. Remember that the key to solving analogies is to be a good detective. Some of the other answer choices are related to clocks and time but not to the relationship *between* clocks and time.

29. B: Wires are the medium that carry electricity, allowing the current to flow in a circuit. Pipes carry water in a similar fashion, so the best choice is *B*. Test takers must be careful to not select Choice *E*, which reverses the relationship between the components. Choices *A, C,* and *D* contain words that are related to one another but not in the same manner as wires and electricity.

30. A: This question pulls from knowledge in social studies class, understanding the basic roles and positions of the three branches of the government. The president serves in the Executive Branch and the Supreme Court Justices serve in the Judicial Branch.

Dear SSAT Middle Level Test Taker,

We would like to start by thanking you for purchasing this study guide for your SSAT Middle Level exa[m]. We hope that we exceeded your expectations.

Our goal in creating this study guide was to cover all of the topics that you will see on the test. We also strove to make our practice questions as similar as possible to what you will encounter on test day. Wit[h] that being said, if you found something that you feel was not up to your standards, please send us an email and let us know.

We would also like to let you know about another book in our catalog that may interest you.

SHSAT

This can be found on Amazon: amazon.com/dp/162845475X

We have study guides in a wide variety of fields. If the one you are looking for isn't listed above, then try searching for it on Amazon or send us an email.

Thanks Again and Happy Testing!
Product Development Team
info@studyguideteam.com

Interested in buying more than 10 copies of our product? Contact us about bulk discounts:

bulkorders@studyguideteam.com

m.

h

.

FREE Test Taking Tips DVD Offer

To help us better serve you, we have developed a Test Taking Tips DVD that we would like to give you for FREE. **This DVD covers world-class test taking tips that you can use to be even more successful when you are taking your test.**

All that we ask is that you email us your feedback about your study guide. Please let us know what you thought about it – whether that is good, bad or indifferent.

To get your **FREE Test Taking Tips DVD**, email freedvd@studyguideteam.com with "FREE DVD" in the subject line and the following information in the body of the email:

　　a. The title of your study guide.

　　b. Your product rating on a scale of 1-5, with 5 being the highest rating.

　　c. Your feedback about the study guide. What did you think of it?

　　d. Your full name and shipping address to send your free DVD.

If you have any questions or concerns, please don't hesitate to contact us at freedvd@studyguideteam.com.

Thanks again!

Made in the USA
San Bernardino, CA
13 November 2018